Democratic Governance in Scandinavia

Noralv Veggeland

Democratic Governance in Scandinavia

Developments and Challenges for the Regulatory State

 Springer

Noralv Veggeland
Inland Norway University of Applied Sciences
Elverum, Norway

ISBN 978-3-030-18272-4   ISBN 978-3-030-18270-0   (eBook)
https://doi.org/10.1007/978-3-030-18270-0

This Springer imprint is published by the registered company Springer Nature Switzerland AG
The registered company address is: Gewerbestrasse 11, 6330 Cham, Switzerland

To Unni

Preface

This book, *Democratic Governance in Scandinavia: Developments and Challenges for the Regulatory State*, has, as its academic focus, the Western regulatory state concept, the transformed Scandinavia welfare state, and policy conflicts and democratic challenges. The regulatory impact analysis of the European standard, the analytical studies of developments and organizational reforms, and the comparative approaches presented in this book have been carried out to develop an understanding of who governs the modern Scandinavian countries in a European integration context.

I refer in this book to Robert A. Dahl's classic political science work *Who Governs? Democracy and Power in an American City* (1989), in which he argues changing democracy forms are a reality in our modern times. I also reference this work because it focuses on my research subjects of renewal of governance structures in modern Scandinavia and the EU. I furthermore analyze the imminent regulatory governance structures versus traditional representative government structures.

I have been conducting research into Scandinavian countries' economic and political development for many years. In this work, I have found that all the Scandinavian countries are becoming regulatory state formations, rooted in European integration. The supernational European Union regulatory bounds have, over time, forced these countries' political and economic direction, leading to good and bad effects on the survival of the countries' traditional universal welfare state model and on the people living in the North. There is a lack of books on this issue.

The writing of this book has been inspired by the author's many years of research and writing on Scandinavia and welfare state matters. I feel that it is important to bring knowledge and alternative perspectives on the subject to the public domain, my hope being that the book can inspire people and academics to discuss important democratic issues. I, in this book, present and discuss the thesis that traditional parliamentary and representative democracy is gravely threatened by the building of unelected arm's-length steering bodies in our polities.

As the author of the book, I would like to take the opportunity to express my deep thanks to my colleagues and the Inland University of Applied Sciences, Lillehammer, who have made it possible for me to write this book. Special thanks must also go to my colleague Professor Dr. Ole Gunnar Austvik. I would also like to thank the publisher, Springer, and in particular Johannes Glaeser for his assistance.

Lillehammer, Norway   Noralv Veggeland
January 2019

Contents

About the Author

Noralv Veggeland is Professor of Public Policy at Inland Norway University of Applied Sciences. He is former Rector of the University. He was Managing Director of Nordic Regional Research Institute, Copenhagen, for four years; twice a long-term visiting professor and lecturer at Massachusetts State University, Amherst, USA; visiting research fellow at the European University Institute, EUI, Florence; and former member of the Norwegian Research Council. The author has an outstandingly long list of national and international publications. noralv.veggeland@inn.no

Chapter 1
Introduction

This book is a monograph of nine chapters. These introductory notes of the first chapter aim to give the reader a pre-understanding of what lies ahead and of the focus and scope of the political-economic elements you will find in this book. The analytical studies of developments and organizational reforms and the comparative approaches presented in "Democratic Governance in Scandinavia: Developments and Challenges for the Regulatory State" have been carried out to develop an understanding of who governs the modern Scandinavian countries. *Regulatory impact analysis* has captured the attention of many political scientists due to its potential to enhance the accountability and transparency of regulatory governance. Regulatory governance in the EU embraces legal acts such as directives, regulations, and decisions; see Appendix 2. EU member states have formally adopted that there is a need for the analysis of institutional, political, and administrative impacts. Only a few have conducted such analysis. This book tries to fill this gap in the literature, in particular for Scandinavia, which is also often referred to as the Nordic region. Chapter 4 is devoted fully to the regulatory impacts, which occur in this region.

All Scandinavian countries are in some ways attached to and obliged to the European Union, either as a full member state (Denmark, Sweden, Finland) or as a European Economic Area (EEA) member state (Norway, Iceland). All the chapters are therefore contextually in some way related to the EU as a mother regulatory state. The EU governance structure is referred to in this book as a regulatory structure that has greatly influenced the Scandinavian countries and caused the change of the national political steering system from a representative democratic government system to a more instrumental-like governance system of regulatory dominance. As Robert A. Dahl states in the preface of his classic political science work "Who Governs? Democracy and Power in an American City" (1989): "*Whatever form it takes, the democracy of our successors will not and cannot be the democracy of our predecessors*". Chapter 5 of my book is dedicated to this issue and therefore titled "Democracy—a Changing Term."

The study in traditional political science of international policy in the years following World War II has tended to use theories that explain policies in terms of

© Springer Nature Switzerland AG 2020
N. Veggeland, *Democratic Governance in Scandinavia*,
https://doi.org/10.1007/978-3-030-18270-0_1

the development of government institutions and the state of law. This, however, overlooked the regulatory effect of international agreements between sovereign national states such as EU, EFTA, WTO, or NATO. The political-economic aspects were also overlooked.

The economic theory created by the famous economist John Maynard Keynes (1883–1946), named Keynesianism when politically adopted, dominated in these years, Keynesian thinking becoming the economic base for social democratic parties all over Europe, including Scandinavia. The Scandinavian universal welfare state was often named the Keynesian welfare state. European integration and the Treaty of Rome of 1956 came on to and set the political agenda in the 1950s. Political economic impact analyses, which emphasized a national government-centered perspective, therefore gained academic focus. So did the political-economic paradigm rooted in Keynesianism, which essentially is the generation of accumulated effective demand in the national economy by central state intervention principles of an active state. The focus also moved to the socio-institutional paradigm of a central state's overall planning responsibility, as deduced from political Keynesianism. Political Keynesianism came to dominate social democratic policy in the aftermath of World War II, and it is still common in Scandinavian academia to talk about "the rise of the Keynesian welfare state" as being closely bound to the enduring Keynesian "central planning state." Government structures dominated the Scandinavian polity until 1980s, when regulatory governance structures arose after the long-term regulatory influence of the supranational EU. However, which political economy framework ruled governments before the change in the 1980s?

One of the main elements of John Maynard Keynes' major macroeconomic theory "General Theory of Employment, Interest and Money" from 1936 was a response to the interwar depression and employment crisis. Keynes promoted the need for government intervention in times of crisis, to "fill the hole" in employment and in particular the lack of demand for labor. Neoclassical liberal economic policies which have an emphasis on public austerity, small government, and privatization dominated prior to Keynes. According to Keynes, the overall political aim should be to generate full employment. Keynes argued that the solution to the Great Depression was to transform the state and the government apparatus to stimulate the economy ("inducement to invest") through the combination of two approaches: a reduction in interest rates (monetary policy) and government investment in infrastructure (fiscal policy) guided by central planning. It was these structures that became the basic ruling government principles in Scandinavia. As stated, these structures became very much challenged by the new governance structures that arose in the 1980s from EU regulations and an international trend of New Public Management (NPM). In the following chapters, it becomes clear from our impact analyses that the emergence of the regulatory state order gravely threatens traditional forms of democracy. I therefore write a lot about the occurrence of new democracy forms, which may be seen as a response to Robert A. Dahl's quote above about future new democracy concepts and transformations.

The following is an outline of the chapters of the book, chapter by chapter, which is given to provide the reader with a better understanding of the monographic approach. We arrange the chapter introductions in a logical academic order.

The substantial introduction starts with Chap. 2: "The Narrative of the Upcoming of the Regulatory State." The internationally renowned Italian Professor Giandomenico Majone offered under the heading of "The Rise of the Regulatory State in Europe" a succinct answer to this: *"Privatization and deregulation have created the conditions for the rise of the regulatory state to replace the dirigiste state of the past"* (see Chapter 1: 1994: 77). He continued to explain that *"Reliance on regulation—rather than public ownership, planning or centralized administration—characterizes the methods of the regulatory state."* This concept, outlined in this chapter, is related to the administrative reforms of government structures in the Scandinavian countries. These welfare states are, historically, fundamentally based on public ownership, planning, and centralized administration, all five countries having been politically conducted by the steady ruling of social democratic governments. Economically they followed Keynesian economics of a high tax burden and a central state friendly approach. This government approach lasted until the 1980s and the 1990s, when the regulatory order came into being, prevailing to today. The Scandinavian Keynesian welfare states, in this change, transformed from central state friendly government policies to free-market friendly policies, which are based on regulatory state governance policies. The policy of today lends responsibility to right-wing governments of Scandinavia, social-democrat parties today also losing support and voters in Europe.

The Scandinavian countries in a European integration context imply, as outlined in the chapters below, the adoption of a social model of the regulatory state order as a victorious reform wave, as described by Majone. However, the adoption of alternative governance structures requires these to be translated in the national context of different administrative traditions in European regions. These changing administrative traditions are introduced in Chaps. 6 and 7.

Chapter 3 more closely addresses "The Regulatory State in the Study of European Governance." The economic roots of the rise of regulatory governance in the European Union are uncovered in this chapter. The Western and Scandinavian states struggled after the great international stagflation crisis of the mid-1970s to reconstruct their economies and to increase the efficiency of public sector institutions so that they could adapt to the pressures of global competition. EU member states were, moreover, increasingly bound to EU regulatory systems and international agreements that pursue mutually beneficial obligations. Free market economy and globalization pressed for regulatory innovations. These institutional innovations and revolutionary reconstructions were the most important developments that led to the European and Scandinavian regulatory state order of today.

New forms of regulation and planning have arisen in the Scandinavian countries. They serve a wide range of social goals of control, management, and change to facilitate efficiency and innovation in both the private and public sectors. The approach in Chap. 3 provides a comprehensive introduction to this diversity. Treating electoral accountability as a necessary institutional precondition for democratic legitimacy is, however, common sense. In the EU, i.e., the enlarged European Economic Area (EEA), the passing of laws and the publication of EU directives and programs have increased dramatically, as noted in Appendix 2 of this book. Far-reaching laws and powers of authority have come to dominate Western polities. Management through objectives, programming, measurements of goal attainment, quality-securing systems of measurement, reporting, and auditing actions have also been adopted. All these are typical steering instruments of and are supported by the ideals of New Public Management (NPM). These trends are closely analyzed, plausible explanations of new governance elements being given.

Chapter 4 is a specific Scandinavian impact analysis. This chapter analyzes the rise and the concept of the regulatory state in Europe and its impact on Scandinavian democratic welfare state governance. Analysis studies usually are comparative studies of different government structures, in this case in Scandinavia and the EU. Here, we study the transition of the national state order in the wake of the change from government to dominant non-parliamentarian regulatory democratic governance. The universal welfare state is, despite prevailing and costing the taxpayers a huge amount of money, undermined by regulatory interventions. The welfare state is considered to be common sense and has government support. This support is, however, conditional and dependent on commercial market values as the outcome, no longer solely being based on the production of collective welfare goods for all. The welfare state has become regulatory, to guarantee steering by objectives and to make privatization an administrative option. Privatization and market making have become dominant, public services getting new organizational forms that make them more similar to private sectors enterprises, these organizational forms being the so-called arm's-length bodies. Such non-parliamentarian bodies regulate and control public and private activities as market actors. A specific problem is, however, social risk such as the development of inequality and regulatory governance being inclined to eliminate transparency, downgrades, and the importance of social forces and bottom-up initiatives. Democratic deficits challenge and confront today's Scandinavia.

Chapter 5 traces the basic classical democratic principle of a sovereign people that elects its representatives and decides its laws. Laws are society implemented by the executive authority and by the government and its administrative apparatus. A judiciary body (the courts of law) furthermore interprets laws and monitors compliance. Parliamentary surveillance of decision-making in unitary states such as the Scandinavian countries is political. The Supreme Court is the judiciary and is entrusted with this task in federal states such as Germany or the USA. The Supreme Court is responsible for preventing the legislative authorities from making decisions that violate the Constitution, the Constitution limiting both judicial and government authority. Post-national democracy and its governance structure are founded on steering by regulations and objectives, as practiced by the EU. Regulatory state democracy can be outlined as being to a great extent based on national and international agreements and partnerships negotiated in a multicentered, multilevel governance system and on laws and judicial regulations. To this should be added the typical market making of public sectors. All these characterize Scandinavian countries attached to the EU. There constitutionally exists a critical relationship between this and the traditional doctrine of democratic order. This doctrine considers the only form of democratic legitimacy to be linked to elected representative government and national *sovereignty*. The term "democratic deficit" indicates a democratic challenge and is used both academically and politically as a negative perspective on the new forms of regulatory governance. In this chapter, these issues are outlined in a historical perspective, terms and concepts are defined, and the analysis is performed in a Scandinavian setting.

Chapter 6 follows up the political adoption processes behind democratic and governance challenges by introducing "Translation of European Social Models." The national government and governance models found in European countries and their historical traditions are, by and large, still characterized in the Continental and the Scandinavian regions by taxpayer welfare state social economies. The allowance to welfare assets in Great Britain is based on private economic responsibility. The Continental and Scandinavian administrative tradition demonstrates the strong emphasis on balancing pure economic achievements with other goals, such as welfare, employment, social cohesion, leisure, and environmental sustainability. We can, however, going beyond the macro-level of the European economic and social model, distinguish three relevant sub-models: the Scandinavian model (also often named the Nordic model), the Anglo-Saxon, and the Continental type of model. The Mediterranean and a new Eastern Europe model could also be recognized. They are, however, not so important in our study.

The regulatory Anglo-Saxon and the Scandinavian/Nordic models have become quite similar in the nature of relations between governments and markets, for example use of market-type mechanisms to provide government services. They are, however, very different when it comes to the size of government and state-centered planning and distributive policies. The central state friendly Scandinavian welfare state policy, however, proceeds even though a transformation process approaching that of the Anglo-Saxon model and small state and market-making tradition might be recognized.

The Scandinavian/Nordic and the Continental models are more alike in terms of the size of the public sector, job security policies, and trade union relations, but very different in terms of government, labor market relations, and employment regulations. There is no sign of an approaching process. The Anglo-Saxon tradition has ruled the EU so far. What will happen after the United Kingdom's Brexit is currently unknown.

The Scandinavian/Nordic model can accordingly, and despite differences, be said to emerge as a blend of the two large European models. The Anglo-Saxon model's emphasis is on economic liberalism and regulation, and the Continental model's emphasis is on a large public sector and close relations to the labor market organizations. According to the OECD, Scandinavian/Nordic governance has been transformed and has become a regulatory state, a transformation that has not taken place in the EU member states that belong to the other European governance tradition. The OECD, however, states that this transformation seems to be strongly aberrant comparatively. We therefore should look more closely at administrative and management historical traditions.

Chapter 7, "Administrative Traditions and the 'trilemma,'" provides an explanation rooted in historical facts. The term "trilemma" plays a central role and refers to "spill-over" processes forming policy making in the European Union and Scandinavia. "Spill-over" processes and the concomitant increase in mutual dependence between an increasing number of actors have become predominant. The chapter briefly describes, in our context, the trade-offs of equality, full employment and public expenses as being the objectives of the European welfare states. These objectives are, however, incommensurable. Policies might achieve two of them but absolutely not all three. This is the "trilemma."

Trade-offs in the liberal welfare-state political course include, as pointed out previously, the Anglo-Saxon administrative tradition weighing market solutions and regulatory measures and the explicitly expressed objective for the service sector of lessening state intervention. Universal welfare and health coverage are not guaranteed by public arrangements. Employers provide workers with health and social insurance, while the government covers health expenses for the poor and the elderly who fall outside the insurance system. In this tradition, the response to the equality–employment trade-offs was to give priority to job creation and labor-market flexibility while reducing job protection and social security.

The trade-offs in the Corporatist welfare state political course include the Continental administrative tradition depending on corporative solutions and state-interventionist measures. Health and social insurance are guaranteed for all by law, although social insurance is a mixture of public and private institutional arrangements. Traditional welfare services are kept in the public domain as "services of general interest." Trade unions are strong. Too few jobs are, however, created under this administrative tradition. Anglo-Saxon tradition policies have, in recent years, influenced the Continental countries and the Scandinavian countries.

The trade-offs in the universal welfare state political course include the Scandinavian administrative tradition relying on public institutional solutions for social equality, interventionist measures and universal welfare services, and public health and social insurance arrangements as goals and means for the building of social capital. Institutional changes have created public innovations. Indirect governance by regulation due to the use of NPM in the public sector, through outsourcing and contracting out arrangements and the selective reorganization of public administration to public-law agencies (PLAs) and private-law bodies (PLBs), has since the 1980s become common and trade-union power has diminished. The influence of the EU regulatory state is obvious in these processes, though conflict making. Government ruling defines electoral accountability as a necessary institutional precondition for both input- and output-oriented democratic legitimacy. Non-parliamentary governance, however, does not operate in this way.

In Chap. 8 "Conflicting Economic Politics," conflicts are in focus and are outlined in relation to political economics. The reasons for the conflicts are many. One obvious reason, however, is that Scandinavian countries based their universal welfare state model on state friendly Keynesian economic principles. These principles have become eroded since the 1980s by the heavy influence of Anglo-Saxon neoliberalism and administrative tradition. The Scandinavian countries are, in some ways, in a sort of vacuum. They still lack a basic economical alternative to the anti-statist neoclassical economic theory and policy, the ideology manifesting as the aberrant Scandinavian neoliberalism of today. The contemporary theory and policy approach referred to as neo-Keynesian is in contrast to this theory and policy. The neo-Keynesianism approach possibly gives social democratic politics an economic option for Scandinavian countries. As the name suggests, it builds on the economist Keynes's momentous theory from 70 years ago. The chapter analyzes the possible future and conflicts of a possible political economic turn to neo-Keynesianism.

Chapter 9 provides an example of the regulatory turn in a particular economic policy area. The chapter, "Case study: Accounting reform—in the regulatory Norway," relates to the case of Scandinavia and revolves around accounting reform and making public sector institutions more business-like. Business accounts focus on the profitability effect of revenues and expenditures. The profitability effect refers to profitability in the form of revenues (accrued revenues) and profitability in the form of expenditures (investments). This entails two-dimensional accrual accounting. A profitability accrual principle is introduced, which is in addition to the money accrual principle. The profitability accrual principle, which is often referred to imprecisely as the accrual principle, is used to report the profitability effect of both revenues and expenditures. The selection of an accounting model by Scandinavian states for use in the public sector has traditionally been based on a political desire to sustain control of government bureaucracy. The introduction of business-oriented accounting in the public sector has, however, weakened the opportunity for control. Why, then, this reform? The chapter suggests the following answers to accounting in the public sector.

A political perception has arisen, in the framework of the Scandinavian regulatory state, that the public sector should be governed and regulated to the greatest possible extent in the same way as the private sector. There is therefore a need to prepare the same type of accounts that are prepared by the private sector (business accounts in other words). Politicians adopted this reform due to insufficient knowledge of what business accounts represent, and insufficient knowledge of the alternatives that exist for business accounts to ensure regulatory order continues in Scandinavian public sectors (Appendices 1 and 2).

References

Dahl, R. A. (1989). *Who governs? Democracy and power in an American city*. New Haven: Yale University Press.

Majone, G. (1994). The rise of the regulatory state in Europe. *West European Politics, 17*(3), 77–101.

Chapter 2
The Narrative of the Upcoming Regulatory State

Introduction

Scholars sometimes formulate a wide definition of the regulatory concept with reference to societal values. Phillip Selznick (1985: 363) has, for example, provided an uncritical understanding of regulation that is of particular relevance. He states that the central meaning of regulation "...refers to sustained and focused control exercised by a public agency over activities that are valued by a community." He, however, neglected all policy impacts. A clear political science perspective characterizes Fabrizio De Francesco's (2010) analysis. He follows up the regulatory issue through a comprehensive analysis of diffusion and the regulatory impacts in the European Union (EU) and OECD member states. Fritz Scharpf (2019) makes this intervention by treating electoral accountability as a necessary institutional precondition for both parliamentary and regulatory oriented democratic legitimacy, including EU multilevel governance. We intend to critically follow up these approaches in the chapters of this book. Many EU member states, including the Scandinavian countries, have reported that regulatory impact studies either are at the pilot stage or well embedded in their law-making and governance processes. How did the regulatory state arise—what are the narratives?

According to Selznick, the emphasis on valued communal activities is important because regulatory effort helps to uphold public standards, ethics, and norms. He underestimates, however, at the start of the 1980s the power concentration proceedings and rise of the regulatory state in the European domain. This process is analyzed by the OECD in terms of new concept generations that are relevant to Scandinavia, as in OECD (2005), *Guiding Principles for Regulatory Quality and Performance*, and in OECD (2007), *Government Capacity to Assure High Quality Regulation in Sweden.*

OECD and research conceptualization indicates that, in its widest sense, we can define regulation and the implementation of it by government as the totality of all mechanisms of social protection and control (Croley 1996). We find embedded

© Springer Nature Switzerland AG 2020
N. Veggeland, *Democratic Governance in Scandinavia*,
https://doi.org/10.1007/978-3-030-18270-0_2

consequences of this type of defined governance, the regulatory state, to be a growing surveillance and control bureaucracy and a democratic deficit.

According to the theory of the regulatory state, the task of research is to present national and international "narratives" of different institutional arrangements and of the practice of regulatory governance. Alongside this approach is the view of networking theory, which emphasizes the study of partnership agreements as part of political economics. Taming the undemocratic power of the regulatory state issue will probably be essential for future pro-democratic politics (Veggeland 2009). Too much regulation is also an obstacle to economic innovation and may lead to recession.

Mechanisms

Two British scholars, Christopher Hood and Ruth Dixon (2015), both from the University of Oxford, recently published the report: "A Government that Worked Better and Cost less?—Evaluating Three Decades of Reform and Change in UK Central Government." Their conclusion is clear. New Public Management (NPM) and more regulation lead to higher public costs, more complaints, and less parliamentary democracy. Their conclusion caused worldwide debate, as we intend to follow up in our impact analysis. The present EMU regime must be able to control and override the exercise of national governing powers by democratically accountable national governments.

What does a regulatory state order mean, with regard to NPM reforms and contemporary politics? The internationally well-known Italian political economist Giandomenico Majone, under the heading of "The Rise of the Regulatory State in Europe," offered an early and succinct answer: *"Privatization and deregulation have created the conditions for the rise of the regulatory state to replace the dirigiste state of the past"* (1994: 77). He continued to explain: *"Reliance on regulation—rather than public ownership, planning or centralized administration—characterizes the methods of the regulatory state."*

We can, however differentiate these mechanisms. In our context, there are four explanatory conceptions of regulatory management that can be put forward.

1. Law-directed conception: regulation as authoritative rules
2. Economics-directed conception: regulation as efforts of state agencies to manage the economy
3. Politics-directed conception: regulation as mechanisms of steering and management control
4. Sustainability-directed conception: regulation as a means to handle environment threats and the "risk society of the new modernity" (Beck 1992).

These conceptions point to an evolution from a narrow, judicial notion of regulation to a much broader one that accounts, in both theory and practice, for values and agreed normative actions. The present supranational EU regime, as both we and Fritz Scharpf (2019) propose, should be able to control and override the exercise of normative national governing powers by democratically accountable national governments.

In the regulatory state, the concepts of regulation as authoritative rules and agreed normative action lead to the important distinction between "*hard regulation*" and "*soft regulation.*" Hard regulation requires legal actions and mechanisms of enforcement to bring about adherence and sanctions when there is a failure to comply (May 2002). On the other hand, the use of soft regulation, sometimes viewed as regulation through persuasion and deliberative discourse, has the aim of agreement as the preferred outcome (Streeck 1995, Amdam and Veggeland 1998). Soft regulation turns to deliberative solutions (McGowan and Wallace 1996) and allows not strictly legally binding commitments to be made between parties, which give actors more leeway on how to achieve regulatory goals and development objectives (Mörth 2004).

The soft-regulatory strand comprises guidelines and various forms of encouragements to achieve desired outcomes. This approach, however, means that the rules can for example be different in different countries, as long as it is possible to determine that the rules fulfill the agreed upon common objectives. This is deliberate agreement-based regulation, which the European Union has termed "the open method of coordination" since the launch of the Lisbon Process in 2000. Soft regulation, briefly formulated, connotes the following (Veggeland and Elvestad 2008).

- Deliberative work on identifying both the "best solutions" and the "best practices"
- An approach based on the exchange of information and the sharing of development programs
- Mutual confidence and some sort of compatibility between regulatory systems
- A high degree of institutional interaction between regulators
- The foundation of the networking and partnership-building society (Castells 1996; Veggeland 2003)

The wider concept of regulation indicates two basic claims, namely, the organizational change of public institutions and making embracing agreements and control arrangements the condition for the rise of the regulatory state. Reliance on regulation rather than on public ownership, planning, or bureaucratic administration indicates, according to Fritz Scharph, that the methods of this form of state bias the minimization and/or marketization of the public sector, which in turn leads to regulatory governance (Pollitt and Bouckaert 2004). Regulatory governance indicates a shift of the traditional governmental apparatus to a variety of New Public Management (NPM) institutional and structural forms. These are often contextually bound to social models and administrative traditions that interpret regulatory measures differently (Knill 2001; Djelic 2006).

This wider concept indicates that there is an aspect of political economy to this regulatory state method, namely the *institutional-replacement* element, as mentioned in the quotation by Majone above (1994). According to Selznick (1985), the goal of this method is to achieve what is "valued by a community." We, however, need *criteria and guidelines* by which we can assess whether or not institutional replacements and innovations have led to what is valued. Indications of the general consequences of transformed social-institutional paradigms, furthermore, imply new social risks as we advance toward a new modernity (Taylor-Gooby 2004). How can we avoid regulations that generate vulnerability and counteract the risks? How can the regulatory state be tamed? What is valued by a community and what can a community consider to be either a success or a failure, or ethically good or bad? We aim here to address these vital questions by employing an exploratory and critical perspective. Such an approach to the study of the arrival and the rise of the contemporary regulatory state should contain the following six elements.

- Basic conditions and an analysis of political economy
- Methods and mechanisms
- Social models and administrative traditions
- Institutions and structural replacements
- Basic institutional impacts
- Efforts, criteria, and guidelines which help to tame the regulatory state and uphold public standards and good governance (Olsen 2005)

The commencement of the regulatory state certainly meant an embracing of institutional innovation in the Western world (Veggeland 1999, 2008). Our approach views innovation not only as the application of new institutional solutions to the new international and national economic problems which arose in the wake of the 1970–1980s stagflation crisis, but also as new solutions to old problems such as overloaded public budgets and the hollowing out of government (McCracken et al. 1977).

Regulatory innovation is therefore here understood as sustained attempts by governmental institutions to alter the behavior of others indirectly through law, standards, goals, partnerships, and contracts, and also through creating new implementing and controlling institutions and bodies. Contextually, we are talking about here the methods of regulatory governance, the use of the principles and measures of New Public Management (NPM), market-type mechanisms (MTMs), and arm's-length bodies in the public sector and legal control (OECD 2002; Lane 2000). These mechanisms and bodies need either to be established by taking advantage of deregulation or need to be controlled and tamed by re-regulation. New benchmarking institutions, quality-securing and output-measuring systems, judiciary powers, surveillance agencies, and not least the independent Central Bank are the new institution innovations that characterize the regulatory state order, the independent national Central Bank being organized as a governmental arm's-length body in the framework of a non-Weberian bureaucratic and non-interventionist style (Veggeland 2004a).

The monetarist economic regime, which authorizes the independent central bank to regulate the flow of money in the macro-economy, is another significant element of this style and of the regulatory state (Stewart 1972; Friedman 1962). The central bank regulates profits, investments, and wages in a supply-side directed economy through decisions on interest rates and currency measures, with the view of balancing inflation and aggregated employment. Parliament sets the upper and lower limits for the inflation rate, but is excluded from the implementation of its decisions. The bank is responsible for decision execution.

The driving force behind the methods of regulatory governance are the intention of enhancing the ability to compete more effectively in the global age, producing tangible outcomes and reducing risks, all of which involve mechanisms of standards-setting, information-gathering, benchmarking, and behavior modification in an increasingly vulnerable society (Beck 1992; Black 2005). National implementations of the regulatory state methods do not necessarily create convergent developments nor reduce risks. The methods as organizational ideas are in general influenced by path-dependent interpretations and become diversified. This tendency occurs because of the different European social models and administrative traditions, these changing the contextual framework and thereby the ideas themselves (Røvik 2007). Later chapters will place this tendency in a Scandinavian context.

It is often said that changes of social-institutional paradigms always have backgrounds that are marked by specific economic crises. Crises in the techno-economic system in particular deeply affect institutional order, crises such as the stagflation crisis of the 1970–1980s. We shall return to this political economic crisis later. However, we for now can mention that, at this stage, new techno-economic crises seem always to arise without much being known from economic theory about their socio-institutional impact. Such knowledge arises in the aftermath.

One actual upcoming crisis appears to be the sharp global rise in food prices, in particular the prices of rice, corn, and grain, which have risen by 50–100% and more since the 1980s. People who are very dependent on such staple foods and live in poor countries tend to be deeply and adversely affected by this. It is therefore not at all surprising that these conditions lead to turbulence. Hence, we see extensive rioting and upheavals in many countries around the world today.

What has happened? We can find one main cause of rising food prices and of the crisis in changes within the techno-economic system. Cultivated land for food production has all around the world been transformed by re-regulatory acts that front sustainable developments into land for the production of biofuels. The motivation behind this change in production has been the fear of an imminent global warming caused by the increase of atmospheric carbon dioxide due to the extensive use of fossil fuels.

The economist Erik S. Reinert (2008) 10 years ago introduced a noteworthy approach to the food crisis. He contextualizes the current food crisis by referring to the simple exchange economy that exists among certain indigenous people living in the Pacific. Fish, vegetables, fruits, and ordinary everyday utilities were exchanged in a system that was different from the exchange system for prestigious items, such as canoes or gold. Exchanges of the prestigious items were protected by ceremonies and could not be obtained through the exchange of food. Such a divide existed until recently also in Western economies, food markets being divided from energy markets. The global economy has, however, broken this taboo of division. Biofuels destined for the rich part of the world and its relentless consumption of luxury compete directly with the food resources of the poorest. This disrupts ethical values negatively and challenges politics. What we are, altogether, witnessing is a crisis that is arising out of technological replacement and thereby substantial changes in the system of economic exchange. This in turn heavily influences the socio-institutional order worldwide.

In this impact analysis, we examine the historical crises, changes, and risks that have led to the arrival of this now threatened regulatory state and the mechanisms and aspects constituting the challenges faced by this kind of state. We will also analyze which mechanisms threaten the socio-institutional balance and which are supposed to have taming or moderating effects (Veggeland 2004a, b, 2007; Iversen 2005; Held and Koenig-Archibugi 2003; Iversen and Wren 1998).

The Regulatory State: Risk and Policy Style

Let us first discuss the origins of the regulatory socio-institutional mode of state formation (Osborne and Gaebler 1993; Dyson 1980). Top-down national state intervention, macroeconomic stabilization, income redistribution, market regulation, and central public planning characterized the dominant model of central planning in Western states in the first two decades after the Second World War. The prescript for this was inspired by the political economy deduced from the theory of John Maynard Keynes (1883–1946) and the ideology of Keynesianism. Government institutions were organized hierarchically and were, due to a Weberian bureaucratic structure, given the responsibility to implement Keynesian policies. Economic growth in Western European countries and Scandinavia was strong, and their national economies were relatively locked out from the international market movement. Bureaucratic control and public ownership were important elements of state regulation, and the power of the central government was little disputed (Millward 2000; Majone 1996).

The international economic crisis, which began in the 1970s, led to a demand for new forms of government and governance other than Keynesian central planning and traditional government management. The new model of governance by objectives and market making of public services in the public domain was dominated by neoliberal ideas calling for increased competition in both free markets and public sectors. Welfare state reforms and deregulation became political keywords and, with Keynesian prescriptions, out of the political agendas (Friedmann 1987; Majone 1997). Management by objectives replaced bureaucratic government control, frameworks of deregulation having been regarded as the most characteristic trait in this model.

Paradoxically, this period also introduced an incredible increase in the number of new regulations and the extension of regulative policies, these also reaching new areas, as statistically indicated in Appendix B. This expansion occurred at both national and European (EU) levels and included Scandinavia (Tranøy 2006; Moran

2003; Hooghe and Marks 2001). Yet, this paradox was no more than apparent. The traditional forms of regulation, planning, and control collapsed under the pressure of both new technological advances and the new economic and ideological forces arising out of globalization. This process has been called deregulation. This concept is, however, used in such a manner that it creates the wrong impression. There has definitely not been any reduction in public regulation in the direction of laissez-faire. Instead, what has taken place is the implementation of policies based on a combination of deregulation and re-regulation at different levels of policies and management, deregulation being for the purpose of meeting the demands of the new market and re-regulation being for market-correcting objectives and the promotion of human, social, and environmental rights (Scharpf 1999). In short, new forms of top-down planning and regulation have replaced the old ones. These new forms are also growing at a quicker rate than their predecessors are being removed (Majone 1997).

Generally, regulation defines governmental or state interference with market and globalization processes. However, we should do well at this stage to define more accurately the term "risk regulation," because it is a part of a rather complex web of policy concepts. There are at least two approaches to the term: a risk approach (Beck 1992; "The Risk Society") and an institutional style approach as clearly defined by G. Majone (Majone 1994; "The Regulatory State").

1. *The risk approach*: For our purposes, this term may refer to two different policies: a differentiated, technical, particular case-orientated policy aimed at the reduction of risk and problem-solving actions or an institutional change-orientated policy that inadvertently creates new risks and negative externalities (Taylor-Gooby 2004). Examples of the latter might be increasing transactional costs as a repercussion of governmental fragmentation (Scharpf 1997) or increasing vulnerability because of expanding international interdependence and the network economy.
2. *The institutional-style approach*: This approach refers to the emergence of the state role as regulator, which has advanced rapidly since the 1970s (Majone 1997, 2003). The traditional roles of the state as direct employer, property owner, and service producer have since then declined through privatization and arm's-length agencies and bodies. The use of regulatory measures entails both indirect state governance and the creation of new regulatory institutions, the institutional style of the regulatory state consisting of organizational policy, the creation of adaptive agencies and bodies, and legal surveillance and control policy. Policies aim to extend the regulatory state order of institutions and mechanisms (Beetham et al. 2002).

Here we examine risks and, in a political and ethical perspective, how to moderate those risks with the analytical partitions and the following as points of departure.

(A) Institutional, change-orientated, regulatory policy of intention creates unintended new risks and negative externalities.

(B) Institutional style of the regulatory state comprises organizational change policy, the creation of adaptive arm's-length agencies and bodies, and connected legal surveillance and control policy.

(C) Both the inclination toward institutional risk and policies that seek socioeconomic security represent a combination that figures as a major driving force behind regulatory growth, for example, in the development of the numerous EU regulations (Veggeland 2007).

(D) A policy for taming the regulatory state generates a wide range of new regulations, ethical and "soft" regulations as well as legal and "hard" regulations.

Part of this framework for regulatory policy is the global network economy, so meaning increasing international competition (Castells 1996). At least, two characteristic features have appeared that require regulation in the wake of the arising network economy. A new organization of enterprises, often termed the "post-Fordist" style, emerged in the 1970s and began to dominate the industrial sector. Smaller networking enterprise entities were made competitive through customized and flexible specialization (Storper and Scott 1992; Amin 1994) and trade with services across borders increased heavily and pulled public services into global markets. This pushed public services toward organizational reforms that featured fragmentation, the principles of New Public Management, and the establishment of arm's-length bodies to target competitiveness (Pollitt and Bouckaert 2004; Veggeland 2003). These two things created, and continue to create, on the one hand an increasing need for international market enlargements through deregulation and, on the other hand, the need to re-regulate for a host of different reasons, such as the correction of market imperfections, the steering of actors through regulatory means, agreements, contracts, regulatory consumer protection, and sustainability.

The regulatory state concept enjoyed a high state of legitimacy in Europe toward the end of the previous century. Politically, the question was raised. EU legislation, however, could draw upon the democratic legitimacy of national governments and the potential ability of the supranational EU regime to control and override the exercise of national governing powers by democratically accountable regulatory efforts. This was visible, among other things, in the political changes in many European countries. In the 1990s, elected social-democratic governments replaced the market-liberal governments of the 1980s, as in the United Kingdom and Scandinavia. Social-democratic parties have traditionally distanced themselves, both ideologically and politically, from the liberal and conservative parties, and have placed a greater emphasis on public planning and regulatory control (Giddens 1998).

Revisiting Majone's Concept of the Regulatory State

Giandomenico Majone has called the new institutional form of state a regulatory one. This form appeared at the end of the 1970s and expanded "the regulatory state," it rising in Europe in the wake of the European integration that began in the 1950s.

Majone considers the European Union to be a prime example of this form of a regulatory state order (Majone 1990, 2003). The form is characterized ideologically by neoliberalism, institutionally by frenetic innovation inclination (Moran 2003) and socially by anti-interventionism and liberal welfare reforms (Iversen 2005; Veggeland 2007). Characteristic traits of the new form of state include the deregulation of markets and the decentralization of steering capacity, with ever more networking abilities and multilevel governance.

Equally important for our purpose is Majone's (1990) identification of the paradoxical development that has accompanied this period, this featuring much talk about deregulation and a free market orientation. There has been a dominant tendency toward the growth of a comprehensive policy of regulation and strategic planning at all tiers, the European, national, and regional. On reflection, this is not so surprising. Traditional forms of regulation and control, inherited from the interventionist state of Keynesianism, have broken down in the face of powerful technological, economic, and ideological forces. The techno-economic paradigm has changed radically (Millward 2000). New forms of regulation and institutional planning paradigms needed to be developed to serve other and different political and social goals of control and management.

The passing of laws and the publication of directives increased dramatically, wide-reaching laws, regulations, and legal agreements dominating. The new form of regulatory governance gained its legitimacy, strictly speaking, from legality and goal attainment, and only very indirectly from decision-making institutions of representative democratic assemblies (Schmitter 2000; Scharpf 1999). Institutional benchmarking instruments prioritized the evaluation of results, replacing bureaucratic administration control. Strategic planning is part of this system, because the attainment of goals and the achievement of results require increasingly more extensive and thorough planning than reforms based on the standardized, patterned activities of the interventionist state claimed by market initiatives. In this regulatory system, each individual, group, and business activity must be planned in a way that the setting of goals and the evaluation of results become practical possibilities (Veggeland 1999).

Europeanization processes furthermore brought about pressure through integration processes, the EU as a complete regulatory state pushing member states in the same direction. Member states came under supranational regulatory governance. For example, the French Conseil d'Etat has calculated that the national government issues only 20–25% of all legally binding norms applicable in France, without any prior consultation in Brussels. An analogous situation presumably prevails in all other member states (Lavenex and Wallace 2005). This trend is also visible in the Scandinavian EU states and in the EEA[1] country of Norway. It is reported that from 1995 to 2018 more than 12,000 legally binding EU legal acts have become

---

[1]European Economic Agreement (EEA). Norway is member of the European Free Trade Association (EFTA) but is outside of the EU. EFTA negotiated forward the EEA with the EU in the early 1990s, which Norway signed and implemented in 1995.

Norwegian laws and rules. A large proportion of EU laws and regulations are decided and defined as legal acts, which are to be implemented nationally. There are three named types of legal acts: directives, regulations, and decisions (see Appendix B). These legal acts are, in a national law-making process, adopted and tailored to fit existing rules and norms of the polity in each of the member states. The laws devised to regulate the market for the free flow of goods, services, capital, and labor to a large degree, therefore, make new demands on forms of market-orientated strategic planning at all administrative levels (Hayward and Menon 2003).

The concept of deregulation in the sense of eliminating rules therefore is misleading. As Majone (1997: 143) has noted, new forms of re-regulation follow in the wake of deregulation.

> What is observed in practice is never a dismantling of public regulation—a return to a situation of Laissez-faire which never existed in Europe—but rather a combination of deregulation *and* re-regulation, possibly at different levels of governance.

With reference to the regulatory state order, Thierstein (1997) has asserted that it is no longer adequate to focus only on formal political institutions such as elected bodies and the hierarchy of bureaucratic order in the framework of the classical Weberian type. The political system develops a network of hybrid institutions, which are part of the planning and decision-making process at different levels, but operate at arm's-length from the hierarchy. These agencies must be recognized as an integrated part of a political system that is in the process of institutional change (Majone 1997). It has been argued that the concept of "governance," understood as political steering practice based on regulatory agreements between public, semi-public,[2] and private actors in political and planning arenas, captures this wider perspective. Europe integrates through a combination of the efforts made by local, regional, national, and supranational actors. These actors can be either public or private (Thierstein 1997). This dimension represents an important starting point in the understanding of the transformation of the interventionist state.

The notion of democratic deficit has emerged in the wake of agreement-based structures of governance (Chryssochoou 2004; Veggeland 2003). Global market forces and international bodies of regulation and agreements, such as the EU, seem to undermine the power and influence of national parliaments. The legitimacy of this state order appears, therefore, to be under threat (Beetham and Lord 1998).

The critiques that the regulatory state suffers from democratic deficit and the explanations of its strengthening position may often lack an empirical basis. Majone (1997) has, however, still insisted that this deficiency does not lessen the importance of the main issue. What remains at stake is the increasing number of voters who are convinced and willing to support a new model for the governing of their society. This is a model which includes the marketization of the public sector, increased competition in the economy with the risk of failures, greater emphasis on developing

---

[2]Arm's-length public bodies are run in accordance with private law.

the supply side of the economy, and vast reforms of the welfare state (Pollitt and Bouckaert 2004; Beetham and Lord 1998).

Such forms of regulation create the need for a detailed knowledge of and active joint participation in processes of governance at all levels. Majone (1997) has also pointed out that this factor, in addition to giving market actors and lower tiers of the administrative hierarchy greater responsibility, has led to the establishment of specialized public and private partnerships and semi-public (hybrid) companies. Their tasks are connected with the collection of information, the development of objectives, the supervision of the implementation of project, and joint participation in the management and the evaluation of results. Such agencies and institutions operate outside the line of organization and outside the hierarchical control or supervision of the central authorities. Typical traits in the regulative form of state are, according to Majone, as follows (1997: 146).

> Administrative decentralization and regionalization; the breakdown of formerly monolithic entities into single-purpose units with their own budgets; delegation of responsibility for service delivery to private, for profit or not-for-profit, organizations, and to non-departmental bodies operating outside the normal executive branch framework. Competitive tendering and other contractual or quasi-contractual arrangements whereby budgets and decision making powers are devolved to purchasers who, on behalf of their client group, buy services from the supplier offering the best value for money.

What distinguishes the regulatory model from the traditional, bureaucratic model are the emphasis on discretionary decision-making rather than on rule-governed decision-making and the combination of expertise and independence with specialization within a relatively narrowly defined area of regulation and activity. The institutions operate at a distance from the central authorities and are only indirectly under democratic control; they are "unelected" (Vibert 2007). Majone (1997) has argued as though this model were unconditionally superior to more traditional methods of making and implementing policy.

There are, however, numerous arguments that oppose this view (Veggeland 2003; Le Galès 2003; Sachs 2006). Some argue that distributive policies, or policies with significant redistributive implications, for example, should remain under direct democratic control and Weberian bureaucratic executives. The regulatory model is most relevant in commercial sectors, i.e., private sectors, where economic mechanisms and competition instruments are used. It is also relevant as public arm's-length bodies under private law, an organizing principle for market making of public activities, where market expertise, flexibility, and reputation are keys to greater effectiveness.

The arm's-length bodies and agencies of the regulatory state, committees, and corporations are important because of their inherent specialized knowledge and the possibility of making credible policy commitments. Majone (1990) underlines, however, that the real comparative advantage of agencies is the combination of expertise and long-term commitment.

Long-term policy commitment is notoriously difficult to achieve in a democracy, which is a form of government pro tempore. The time limit imposed by the requirements to hold elections at regular intervals is a powerful constraint on the arbitrary use of the powers entrusted to the winners of the electoral contest by the voters. The segmentation of the democratic process into relatively short periods of time has, however, serious consequences whenever the problems faced by society require long-term solutions. Political principals can transfer power to their agents within limits set by law, but cannot transfer legitimacy in the same way. The new institutions have to achieve their own legitimacy.

McGowan and Wallace (1996) have asserted that the paradigm followed by the regulatory state, based on management by objectives and independent arm's-length agencies, is expressed differently in institutional terms in Western countries. Their view agrees with the approach of path-dependence forming that runs from a diversity of social models and administrative traditions (Knill 2001). For this reason, the regulatory state of the EU does not one dimensionally create administrative convergence in Europe. More often the resulting outcome is divergence (Page and Wouters 1995).

Let us consider some examples.

The comprehensive and deep-reaching planning required in steering by goals varies in dimensions from country to country. McGowan and Wallace have noted that in the USA, with its traditional skeptical approach to planning, the ability to regulate has been developed and has been based on the judiciary and the courts being used to control the implementation and results of regulatory policies rather than independent agencies.

In Japan, on the other hand, regulation is based on strategic planning. We must not equate the Japanese view of the planning paradigm in terms of the paradigm of the Communist planned economy. Instead, planning focuses on particular sectors, promoting swift development and growth, preparing the ground for foreign investment, ensuring state finance, and devising a suitable trade policy (Itoh 1992).

In this regard, the social democracies in Nordic and Continental Europe seem closer to the Japanese approach, perhaps going even further in their enthusiasm for public-planning actions. The culture of the social-democracy states has, however, been developed over a long period and favors planning at all levels and within all sectors. Highlighting differences does not mean that a convergence of the different models and paradigms will not occur in the long term (Veggeland 2007).

Let us summarize very briefly. Majone (1997: 148) has provided an overview of the key traits that distinguish the interventionist state from the regulatory state order.

According to the theory of regulation, the task of research is to present "small narratives" of different institutional arrangements and the practice of governance.

Alongside this approach is the view of networking theory that emphasizes the study of the "politics (of) how to catalyze coordination processes at different levels and how to construct appropriate institutions" (Thierstein 1997: 13).

Taming of the undemocratic power of the regulatory state will be essential for future European and Scandinavian politics.

References

Amdam, J., & Veggeland, N. (1998). *Teorier om samfunnsplanlegging*. Oslo: Universitetsforlaget.

Amin, A. (Ed.). (1994). *Post-Fordism: A reader*. Oxford, UK: Blackwell.

Beck, U. (1992). *Risk society: Towards a new modernity*. London: Sage.

Beetham, D., & Lord, C. (1998). *Legitimacy and the European Union*. London: Longman.

Beetham, D., et al. (2002). *Democracy under Blair: A democratic audit of the United Kingdom*. London: Politico's Publishing.

Black, J. (2005). What is regulatory innovation? In J. Black, M. Lodge, & M. Thatcher (Eds.), *Regulatory innovation: A comparative analysis*. Cheltenham, UK: Edward Elgar.

Castells, M. (1996). *The rise of the network society*. Oxford: Blackwell.

Chryssochoou, D. N. (2004). EU democracy and the democratic deficit. In Helen de Buck & Philippe *The social dialogue and the role of social partners in the EEA*, EFTA Bulletin (pp. 73–78). Brussels: EFTA.

Croley, S. P. (1996). The administrative procedure act and regulatory reform: A reconciliation. *Administrative Law Journal, 10*(1), 35–49.

Djelic, M.-L. (2006). Marketization: From intellectual agenda to global policy-making. In M.-L. Djelic & K. Sahlin Andersson (Eds.), *Transnational governance: Institutional dynamics of regulation*. Cambridge: Cambridge University Press.

Dyson, K. A. (1980). *The state tradition in Western Europe: A study of an idea and institution*. Oxford: Martin Robertson.

Francesco De, F. (2010). *A comprehensive analysis of policy diffusion: Regulatory impact analysis in EU and OECD Member States*. Thesis, University of Exeter.

Friedman, M. (1962). *Capitalism & freedom*. Chicago: The University of Chicago Press.

Friedmann, J. (1987). *Planning in the public domain*. Princeton, NJ: Princeton University Press.

Giddens, A. (1998). *The third way: The renewal of social democracy*. Cambridge: Polity Press.

Hayward, J., & Menon, A. (Eds.). (2003). *Governing Europe*. Oxford: Oxford University Press.

Held, D., & Koenig-Archibugi, M. (Eds.). (2003). *Taming globalization: Frontiers of governance*. Cambridge: Polity Press.

Hood, C., & Dixon, R. (2015). *A government that worked better and cost less? Evaluating three decades of reform and change in UK Central Government*. Oxford: Oxford University Press.

Hooghe, L., & Marks, G. (2001). *Types of multi-level governance*. Producer www. ELOP, Austria.

Itoh, M. (1992). The Japanese model of Post-Fordism. In M. Storper & A. J. Scott (Eds.), *Pathways to industrialization and regional development*. London: Routledge.

Iversen, T. (2005). *Capitalism, democracy and welfare*. Cambridge: Cambridge University Press.

Iversen, T., & Wren, A. (1998). Equality, employment, and budgetary restraint: The trilemma of the service economy. *World Politics, 50*, 507–546.

Knill, C. (2001). *The Europeanization of the national administrations*. Cambridge: Cambridge University Press.

Lane, J.-E. (2000). *New public management*. London: Routledge.

Lavenex, S., & Wallace, W. (2005). Justice and home affaires. In H. Wallace, W. Wallace, & M. A. Pollack (Eds.), *Policy-making in the European Union* (pp. 457–482). Oxford: Oxford University Press.

Le Galès, P. (2003). The changing European state: Pressures from within. In J. Hayward & A. Menon (Eds.), *Governing Europe* (pp. 380–394). Oxford: Oxford University Press.

Majone, G. (Ed.). (1990). *Deregulation or re-regulation?* London: Pinter.

Majone, G. (1994). The rise of the regulatory state in Europe. *West European Politics, 17*(3), 77–101.

Majone, G. (1996). *Regulating Europe*. London: Routledge.

Majone, G. (1997). From the positive to the regulatory state: Causes and consequences of change in the mode of government. *Journal of Public Policy, 17*(3), 139–189.

Majone, G. (2003). The politics of regulation and European regulatory institutions. In J. Hayward & A. Menon (Eds.), *Governing Europe* (pp. 297–312). Oxford: Oxford University Press.

May, P. (2002). *Regulations and motivations: Hard versus soft regulatory paths*. Paper presented, 2002 annual meeting of the American Political Science Association held in Boston.

McCracken, P., et al. (1977). *Towards full employment and price stability*. Paris: OECD.

McGowan, F., & Wallace, H. (1996). Towards a European regulatory state. *Journal of European Public Policy, 3*(4), 560–576.

Millward, A. S. (2000). *The European rescue of the nation-state*. London: Routledge.

Moran, M. (2003). *The British regulatory state: High modernism and hyper-innovation*. Oxford: Oxford University Press.

Mörth, U. (Ed.). (2004). *Soft law in governance and regulation: An interdisciplinary analysis*. Cheltenham, UK: Edward Elgar.

OECD. (2002). *Distributed public governance: Agencies, authorities and other government bodies*. Paris: OECD.

OECD. (2005). *Guiding principles for regulatory quality and performance*. Paris: OECD.

OECD. (2007). *Government capacity to assure high quality regulation in Sweden*. Paris: OECD.

Olsen, J. P. (2005). *Maybe it is time to rediscover bureaucracy?* (Working Paper 10). Oslo: ARENA.

Osborne, D., & Gaebler, T. (1993). *Reinventing government*. New York: Plume.

Page, E., & Wouters, L. (1995). The Europeanization of the national bureaucracies? In J. Pierre (Ed.), *Bureaucracy in the modern state: An introduction to comparative public administration* (pp. 185–204). Aldershot, UK: Edward Elgar.

Pollitt, C., & Bouckaert, G. (2004). *Public management reform: A comparative analysis*. Oxford: Oxford University Press.

Reinert, E. S. (2008). *Matvareboblen*. Klassekampen, Wednesday 30 April 2008.

Røvik, K. A. (2007*). Translasjoner og Trender. Ideer som former det 21. Århundrets Organisasjoner*. Bergen: Fagbokforlaget.

Sachs, J. D. (2006). Welfare states, beyond ideology. *Scientific American*, November 2006, p. 20.

Scharpf, F. (1997). *Games real actors play: Actor-centered institutionalism in policy research*. Boulder, CO: Westview Press.

Scharpf, F. (1999). *Governing in Europe: Effective and democratic?* Oxford: Oxford University Press.

Scharpf, F. (2019). Multilevel democracy: A comparative perspective. In N. Behnke et al. (Eds.), *Configurations, dynamics and mechanisms of multilevel governance*. Cham: Palgrave Macmillan. https://doi.org/10.1007/978-3-030-05511-0_14.

Schmitter, P. C. (2000). *How to democratize the European Union... and why bother?* Lanham, MD: Rowman & Littlefield.

Selznick, P. (1985). Focusing organizational research on regulation. In R. G. Noll (Ed.), *Regulatory policy and the social sciences* (pp. 363–367). Berkeley, CA: University of California Press.

Stewart, M. (1972). *Keynes and after*. Middlesex, UK: Penguin Books.

Storper, M., & Scott, A. J. (Eds.). (1992). *Pathways to industrialization and regional development*. London: Routledge.

Streeck, W. (1995). Neo-voluntarism: A new European social policy regime? *European Law Journal* (1), 31–59.

Taylor-Gooby, P. (Ed.). (2004). *New risks, new welfare. The transformation of European welfare state*. Oxford: Oxford University Press.

Thierstein, A. (1997). *Sustainable regional development: What does it mean for governance?* Paper presented at European regional science association 37th European regional science congress, 26–29 August 1997, Rome.

Tranøy, B. S. (2006). *Markedets makt over sinnene (The Power of the Market over minds)*. Oslo: Aschehoug.

Veggeland, N. (1999). *The arrival of the regulatory state. Global challenge and state response*. Paper. Lillehammer: Lillehammer University College.

Veggeland, N. (2003). *Det nye demokratiet. Et politisk laboratorium for partnerskap*. Kristiansand: Høyskoleforlaget/Norwegian Academic Press.

Veggeland, N. (2004a). The competitive society. In *How democratic and effective?* Kristiansand: Norwegian Academic Press.

Veggeland, N. (2004b). Post-national governance and transboundary regionalization: Spatial partnership formations as democratic exit, loyalty and voice options. In O. Kramsch & B. Hooper (Eds.), *Cross-border governance in the European Union* (pp. 157–170). London: Routledge.

Veggeland, N. (2007). *Paths of public innovation in the global age. Lessons from Scandinavia.* Cheltenham, UK: Edward Elgar.

Veggeland, N. (2008). Path dependence and public sector innovation in regulatory regimes. *Scandinavian Political Studies, 31*(3), 2008.

Veggeland, F., & Elvestad, C. (2008). *International trade and soft regulation: Trade facilitation and regulation programs in Canada and the EU.* Report. Oslo: Norwegian Agricultural Economics Research Institute.

Vibert, F. (2007). *The rise of the unelected. Democracy and the new separation of powers.* Cambridge: Cambridge University Press.

Chapter 3
The Regulatory State in the Study of European Governance

Approaches

I will first begin with the alternative definition of Frank Vibert on regulatory arm's-length bodies, bodies which are already introduced in the former chapter: "Unelected bodies include central banks, independent risk management bodies, independent economies and ethics regulators, regimes of inspection and audit and new types of appeal bodies" (Vibert 2007: 5).

Regulatory measures and regulatory agencies and bodies have, since the 1980s, due to the influence of advice from the Organisation for Economic Co-operation and Development (OECD) and the penetration of regulations from the European Union (EU), burgeoned through the extension of institutional innovations into new areas of national economic and social life. See additional information from the OECD given in Appendix A. The items we buy, the utilities we demand, the work conditions we accept, the welfare services we are offered, and the public management we are subordinate to have become increasingly subject to regulations and legal controls, usually administered by specialized agencies. The institutional self-regulation of the past has been transformed. Markets, societal sectors, organizations, and institutions are deregulated to liberate free market forces and re-regulated to generate controlled state management. Deregulation and re-regulation are together summoned up in our concept of the regulatory state.

Today even knowledge-creating institutions such as universities are now subject to statutory innovations in the form of new regulations, these replacing the traditional self-governance of the "command-and-control" type of bureaucracy (Rhodes 1997). National public administrations organized as a unified, hierarchical state bureaucracy of the Weberian pattern have also been partly replaced. This bureaucracy attempted to manage the whole polity and to pursue the redistribution of resources. It was a process by which the social and individual worlds were increasingly subject to rational action through financial interventions, public monopolies, central planning, formal procedures, and nondiscretionary decision-making. The

© Springer Nature Switzerland AG 2020
N. Veggeland, *Democratic Governance in Scandinavia*,
https://doi.org/10.1007/978-3-030-18270-0_3

state, accordingly, was believed to be building the ability to exercise widespread command and control.

In contrast, the regulatory state stresses legal interventions in the construction of command and control. The approach of "steering without rowing," that is, the withdrawal of the state from both direct participation in the allocation of resources and the role of being owner, has become the general and prevailing idea of dominance.[1] This does not imply withdrawal from steering by regulations. The objective is to correct particular irregularities and market failures through regulatory interventions and to coordinate actions through the regulatory form of negotiated legal agreements and contracts. Fair market competition is also to be protected and promoted. The stress of regulations also spreads to the securing of safety (food, work, health, poverty) and to the diminishing of risks (unknowable in their occurrence and collective in their incidence, pandemics, technology). There furthermore follow legal interventions for the avoidance of discrimination (gender, race, religion, age), the handling of scandals (corruption, risks of business, medical malpractice), the counteracting of and recovery from crises (financial, employment, hunger, malnutrition), the safeguarding of the environment (pollution, global warming, deforestation, etc.), and the programming of cooperation (development programs, research programs, partnerships, etc.) (Hood et al. 2004). The social philosopher Jürgen Habermas (1987) has expressed skepticism to the ever increasing reach of the "systems world" and has argued that we need to protect the privacy of the "lifeworld" through supporting the regulatory state of the EU. This indicates that neither Habermas nor we can ignore the systems world of regulations, and must therefore set the "taming of the regulatory state" on the scholarly agenda (Veggeland 2009).

Roger King (2007: 5), referring to Cass (2005: 60-1), has pointed out the usefulness of distinguishing between "rules" and "regulations." On the one hand, legal "rules tend to be non-discretionary acts of wide application in legally-sustained decision-making"; on the other hand, "regulation, however, although, like rules, also guiding and patterning individual behaviors, tends to be much broader in its sources and in its inclusion of both public and private institutions." Thus, rules provide a high degree of predictability in the realm of management and public administration, much like the intentions behind the bureaucracy described by Max Weber. Regulations, including legal agreements and contracts, should in an economic sense therefore be much more flexible than rules, and are often introduced and modified accordingly to fit changing political economic circumstances. These characteristics are quite unlike the old wisdom on conditional macroeconomic stability, and on stable public management according to Max Weber's neutral and rational bureaucracy.

The term "regulatory state" first came into scholarly use in the study of European politics and the EU through the publication in 1994 of Giandomenico Majone's

---

[1]The financial crisis of 2007/2008, which caused economic recession globally, has returned the state to both allocation and ownership matters through different gigantic governmental packages of different kinds. The prevailing ideology, though, suggests that the involvement is to be temporary.

milestone article, "The Emergence of the Regulatory State in Europe" (Majone 1994). Three years later his next contribution, "The rise of the regulatory state" (Majone 1997),[2] elaborated in detail on the context of the rise of the regulatory state in Europe. Majone observes that traditional forms of bureaucratic regulation and control, inherited from the interventionist state, were being broken down in the face of powerful technological, economic, and ideological forces. Majone also ascribes three major functions to the interventionist Keynesian state: redistribution of resources, economic stabilization, and social regulation. The rise of the regulatory state involves the escalation of the third Keynesian social regulation function, this being at the expense of the other two Keynesian functions, to make social conditions fit into free market principles (Veggeland 2009).

New forms of regulation and social planning have arisen to serve a wide range of social goals and the control, management, and change required to facilitate efficiency and innovation in both the private and public sectors. There has been a dramatic increase in the European Economic Area (EEA) in the passing of laws and the publication of EU directives and programs. Far-reaching laws and powers of judicial authority have come to dominate European polities. The same is true in Scandinavian member states, management through objectives, programming, measurements of goal attainment, quality-securing systems of measurement, reporting, and auditing actions having been adopted. All these are typical steering instruments supported by the ideals of New Public Management (NPM).

Social planning is a part of NPM, but not in the form of traditional, holistic, state central planning. Planning in the regulatory state instead takes place as fragmented strategic acts. This mode of strategic planning benefits market forces and occurs as an independent professional activity in the context of the transformation of self-regulation. Each act must be planned by rules and regulations so that both the achievement of goals and the measurement of results are practically possible. In fact, regulatory action and controls that are meant to facilitate the realization of specific goals and results require more detailed and thorough planning than governance based upon standardized, patterned, and centralized planning activities.

The Western states were struggling, after the great international stagflation crisis of the mid-1970s, to reconstruct their economies and to increase the efficiency of the public sector institutions and through this to adapt to the pressures of global competition. The states were, moreover, increasingly bound to external regulatory systems and agreements that pursue mutually beneficial obligations. These institutional innovations and revolutionary reconstructions were the most important developments that led to the regulatory state of today.

What does the introduction of the regulatory state mean to the contemporary polity? Majone has offered a succinct answer which, due to its fundamental clearness, we repeat frequently in this book: "Privatisation and deregulation have created the conditions for the rise of the regulatory state to replace the dirigiste state of the past" (1994: 77). Furthermore, "Reliance on regulation—rather than public

---

[2]This article of Majone has been cited several hundred times, according to Google Scholar.

ownership, planning or centralized administration—characterizes the methods of the regulatory state."

Other scholars have formulated broader definitions of regulation that invoke either positive or negative societal values. Phillip Selznick, for example, argues that the central meaning of regulation "refers to sustained and focused control exercised by a public agency over activities that are valued by a community," and this role is important because "the regulatory effort helps to uphold public standards, ethics and norms" (Selznick 1985: 363). We come back to Selznick in Chap. 4. On the other hand, Michael Moran has taken a much dimmer view, insisting that "the features of the new kind of state … [are] its persistent interventionism, its drive to ever more systematic surveillance, its colonization of new regulatory spheres … [thus] perversions of its essential purpose" (Moran 2003: 6). Increasing the transactional costs connected to the regulatory state further strengthens this negative perspective (Veggeland 2009). Regulation by agreements and contracting out are part of this regime and relate to network management (Baldwin and Cave 1999: 46). Some researchers have identified two different forms of this kind of management (Kjær 2004: 45).

- One form is "game management," a term which denotes the process of interaction between actors within a network that does not really bring about change within the network. The goal is instead to facilitate agreement from within.
- The other is "network structuring," referring to the changing of the network itself in order to accomplish new goals.

We can define "regulation" in its widest sense as being the totality of all mechanisms of social protection and control (Jordana and Levi-Faur 2004: 3), including its negative repercussions. The EU diversifies the term statistically in Directives, Regulations and Decisions (see Appendix B). Our book addresses this totality of regulatory mechanisms.

In our context, we can put forward five explanatory conceptions of regulation (Baldwin et al. 1998):

1. Law-directed conception: regulation as authoritative rules
2. Economics-directed conception: regulation as efforts of state agencies to manage the economy
3. Politics-directed conception: regulation as mechanisms of steering and democratic control
4. Partnership-directed concept: regulation by agreements and contracts to extend multilevel governance and network coordination
5. Sustainability-directed conception: regulation as a means of eliminating environmental threats and the "risk society of the new modernity" in general (Beck 1992)

These conceptions, as articulated by Baldwin et al., point to an evolution from a narrow, judicial notion of regulation to a much broader one. This is accounted for by both theory and practice and encompasses values and normative and agreement-based actions. This more comprehensive approach, moreover, distinguishes between external and internal regulatory orders and employs comparative analysis to make sense of organizational differences in the translation and implementation of regulatory ideas (Pedersen 2009).

Modes of Regulation

Our focus is on the many aspects of the term regulation and on the presentation of aspects that feature the regulatory power of the EU through an impact analysis approach.

In the regulatory state, the notion of regulation as an assemblage of authoritative rules and agreed normative actions leads to the important distinction between *soft regulation* and *hard regulation*. Both relate to how different regulation techniques can contribute to the functioning of markets, social stability, the reduction of risk, and sustainability.

Hard regulations are EU laws and the statistical terms of EU Regulations and EU Decisions. A "regulation" is a binding legislative act and must be applied in its entirety across the EU. A "decision" is binding on those to whom it is addressed (e.g., an EU country or an individual company) and is directly applicable. For example, if the EU Commission issued a decision on a specific conflicting local case, then the "decision" will be binding on all similar cases in the EU (European Union Info).

Soft regulatory instruments are voluntary mechanisms used to achieve a set of regulatory goals, including the goal of minimizing trade barriers. EU Directives are a form of soft regulation. A "directive" is a legislative act that sets out a goal that all EU countries must achieve. However, it is up to the individual countries to devise their own laws on how to achieve these goals (European Union Info).

Soft regulatory instruments are based on so-called soft law, that is, voluntary documents such as guidelines, declarations, and recommendations. Soft regulatory instruments may also include procedural mechanisms such as benchmarking, open methods of coordination, training programs for regulators, mutual visits and audits, sharing and exchanging information, and the involvement of trading partners as relevant stakeholders in the different stages of regulation.

Soft regulatory instruments from the practical perspective represent alternative uses, including supplements and complements. Hard regulatory instruments represent a set of instruments that is based on binding agreements and mandatory rules. Hard regulation requires legal actions and mechanisms of enforcement to bring about adherence and impose sanctions when there is a failure to comply (May 2002). This approach contrasts with soft regulation, which sometimes is viewed as regulation through persuasion and deliberative discourse, agreement being the preferred outcome (Streeck 1995; Amdam and Veggeland 1998). Soft regulation turns to deliberative solutions (McGowan and Wallace 1996) and allows for commitments between parties that are not strictly legally binding, so giving actors more leeway on how they achieve regulatory goals and development objectives (Mörth 2004).

The soft regulatory strand comprises guidelines and various forms of incentives for achieving desired outcomes. This approach, however, means that the rules can vary, for example, across national borders, providing it is possible to determine that the rules fulfill common objectives. The use of these instruments entails the intentional striving for agreement-based regulations. The European Union has termed this since the launch of the Lisbon Process in 2000 "the open method of coordination." Briefly, soft regulation connotes the following.

- Deliberative work on identifying both the "best solutions" and the "best practices"
- An approach based on the exchange of information and the sharing of development programs
- Mutual confidence and some sort of compatibility between regulatory systems
- A high degree of institutional interaction between regulators[3]
- The foundation of the networking and partnership-building society (Castells 1996; Veggeland 2003)

Trends of Dominance

According to Majone (1997), Baldwin and Cave (1999), Moran (2001), Black (2005), Braithwaite 2008, Veggeland (2009) and other scholars, there are certain key trends that dictate the development of the regulatory state. Four are presented below.

Trend 1: The Use of Legal Authority

The regulatory state's use of legal authority or regulation as supreme tools of policy-making has superseded the Keynesian interventionist-state strategies of stabilization and distribution through the policy of effective demand. As we have already seen, Keynesian interventionist-state strategies attempted to manage the welfare state by using financial and planning measures and through this pursued development, the redistribution of resources, and the provision of social security. The regulatory state, as is constituted by both deregulation and re-regulation, instead stresses legal interventions to create markets through deregulation or to correct markets by re-regulation. The re-regulation embodies new regulations to deal with negative externalities and, in particular, policy failures (Scharpf 1999). The concept of re-regulation normally relates to regulatory innovations (Black et al. 2005), that is,

---

[3]Our approach is a discussion of how regulation is conducted and why it is so important in cases of cross-border cooperation such as the EU.

innovations to take precautions against imbalances, disorders, risks, and threats to safety.

Taking control and introducing such precautions therefore requires innovative policies, and governments now prefer re-regulation as the main tool for these tasks. Ulrich Beck (1992) has introduced the term "risk society" and has claimed that the modern industrial society has a vast range of grave technological, economic, and social risks. The results are unknowable, and incidents have repercussions at a vast collective scale. Pandemics, technological failures, crises of food safety (e.g., bovine spongiform encephalopathy, BSE), systemic crises, and vulnerable communication systems are only just a few examples. As individuals, we can do little to safeguard against these kinds of events. Collectively, however, we can limit their impact through regulatory actions.

Re-regulation is also necessary to facilitate policies that aim to discourage acts of discrimination that relate to ethnicity, gender, race, religion, and age and to combat corruption of every kind, high-risk activities of enterprises, medical malpractice, illegal or uncontrolled migration, social dumping, and regional and urban development. There is a growing focus in the European Union on regulatory measures for migration and immigration. This is due to two factors: the pressure on external borders due to globalization and the pressure on internal borders and welfare arrangements following the integration of the labor markets of 27 member states, some members being wealthy and others poor, plus three states included in the EEA. The standardization of regulations has therefore become complicated. Migration policies affect how immigrants perceive a country, as a country that provides opportunities or as one that sets up obstacles to immigration (van der Velde and van Houtum 2004). This aspect affects not only the number of immigrants and asylum seekers who seek to enter the country, but also the extent to which these immigrants are able to integrate into a society that is very different from the one they came from.

Lastly, there is a need for innovative re-regulation and an institutional ability to avoid and counteract local, national, and international crises such as the financial crisis of the late 2000s and its attendant disorder, imbalance, and risk. There is therefore much talk about the international economic recession and the need for the regulation of financial transactions across borders, state interventions, and credit policies (Stiglitz 2009). Financial crises lead to a dramatic increase in unemployment, negative economic growth, and social imbalance. This very clearly imposes a need to think in new ways about many different issues, not just work, housing, and social-security policies but also, in the economic sphere, interest rates, taxes, and credit policies and, in the political sphere, the role of interventionist versus regulatory policies. Even more so, the persistence all over the world of famines, malnutrition among children, diseases, and poverty leads to demands for a new order of international regulations and conventions. So does the threat of global warming, pollution, and nuclear waste. It is hardly surprising, then, that re-regulation is more than ever a prominent element in proposed solutions to contemporary problems.

Trend 2: The Expanding Role of the EU

The expanding role of the EU's regulatory and monetary policy measures in the absence of other measures (Veggeland 2009), especially the absence of budgetary tools (Majone 1997), facilitates the approach of supranational and intergovernmental regulation by law and derivatives of intergovernmental agreements. The EU is, in a global perspective, an exceptional organization, partly a supranational power and partly an intergovernmental organization (Wallace et al. 2005).

The EU's budget, its financial means, and its capability to develop investments and distribute resources are relatively small compared to the GNP of an average member state. Its budget primarily allocates the financial support provided by the European agriculture and structural policies. The legislative assemblies, the European Parliament and Council of Ministers, and the executive agency, the Commission, can only exercise influence and dominance by working indirectly as regulatory bodies on behalf of the member states. Whatever the limitations it faces, the EU wields its influence effectively through a wide range of acts of deregulation and re-regulation and in manifold scopes and scales. The regulations penetrate administrations at all levels of the European governance system, including the three nonmember countries of the EEA and the European Free Trade Agreement (EFTA), Norway, Iceland, and Lichtenstein.

In other words, the EU facilitates development through regulations, but extends its executive role and displaces its costs down to national and subnational levels. The adoption and implementation of common European regulations does not necessarily create national institutional convergence, divergence normally remaining.[4] This is due to legal acts of directives being subjected to interpretation and tending to be translated in accordance with national frameworks and administrative traditions in a discretionary process that is, of course, under legal surveillance (Knill 2001; Veggeland 2007; Røvik 2007). The member state's translations are innovative and indicate a resistance to copying other member states and a preference for acting in its own interests. The Commission's only opportunity to augment its influence continues to be the expansion of the scope and scale of its regulatory activities and its resources of surveillance. Alternatively, convergence may be achieved by extending "soft regulation," regulation by persuasion, programs, values, and ethics, into the sphere of "hard regulation." We can see this currently happening as a shift from the so-called "hard community method of regulation" to the "soft method of coordination".

---

[4]The scholarly debate on convergence versus divergence in the European Union is a lasting one (Pierre 2001).

Trend 3: The Contributions of Regulators

The regulatory state of the EU inevitably, as more flexible regulation replaces nondiscretionary rule-based governance, becomes intertwined with and dependent upon an array of national "unelected" arm's-length bodies, including civil and nongovernmental regulators (Vibert 2007). In a narrow perspective, these institutions appear limited compared to the building of the many marketized new government bodies and surveillance agencies of the regulatory state (Pollitt and Bouckaert 2004). A wider perspective, however, reveals the regulatory state to be organized and biased in a way that vests responsibility and steering capacity in individual or collective regulators (e.g., professional bodies, boards of arm's-length bodies). This arrangement tends to generate regulatory innovation (Black 2005).

Michael Moran (2001: 21–22), referring to a study of the British regulatory state, explains why and how the "personalization" of regulation has created a corps of high-profile political entrepreneurs (regulators), who have begun to exert an independent influence of their own in setting regulatory agendas. This is an unsurprising outcome, as they rapidly acquire authority and expertise in their regulated area. This development expands the extent and variety of political entrepreneurial approaches and the number of agencies participating in regulatory processes. Regulatory scope and scale are important in the context of facilitating innovative ability (see figure below).

Trend 4: The Audit Explosion

Some researchers have suggested that efforts by the state and the public authorities to regain social control and trust in an era marked by growing institutional innovations also generate risks, vulnerability, and complexity through increased levels of information. This has created the "audit society" (Power 1997), whereby skilled external inspections and controls are replacing internal, self-regulatory, and communicative forms of trusted surveillance and endorsement. The image of the audit explosion describes an accelerating "spillover" process of a neo-functionalistic character (Pollack 2005), which is typical of the emerging regulatory state in the OECD area since the 1980s. The word "audit" relatively recently had connotations of a technical activity that primarily relates to the examination of public budgets and accounts of firms. A satisfactory audit meant an endorsement of honest and responsible activities and a reflection of good management.

The "audit explosion" has transformed this meaning, so that "audit" now refers to an ever expanding activity that seeks to secure good governance and accountability by inspection, not only of public and private finances and budgetary balances, but also in related administrations and in new social sectors. Auditing as a mechanism of the regulatory state appears in social arenas that are as different as universities, health and social care, public service corporations, local government (the Audit of the Municipalities), and national government (the Audit of the Government).

Audits of local and national governments of course still encompass the examination of budgets and accounts. We may, however, wonder what this fairly recent institutional mechanism is. It is supposed to be an inspection of implementations of valued and democratically made decisions and rules, including checking whether the execution of legal decisions is correctly implemented, so that constitutional fraud and failures are avoided.

Municipalities and public service institutions are now bound, in the wake of NPM reforms, to report their achievements of quantitative and qualitative results to regulatory bodies, achievements measured in terms of fixed goals, programs, agreements, and contracts. The rationale for this requirement is twofold, financial according to the concept of result-based allocations and benchmarking according to the concept of determining the winners. Audits of municipalities and the government have an obligation to inspect and check the accuracy of reported data and achievements.

These types of audits clearly represent regulatory innovations. They also, however, considerably expand the basic knowledge of the diversity of arenas. It should also not be overlooked that the expansion of auditing also entails a great expansion of regulatory powers and the creation of new regulatory bodies and departments, which in itself represents institutional innovations.

Trend 5: The Weakening of Corporatist Institutions

In the regulatory state, traditional corporatist institutions no longer meet public decision-makers' need for flexibility. Decision-makers therefore tend to demand greater latitude in the formative process of internal regulations (see Chap. 2) and to negotiate individual social and labor market contracts, thus rejecting collective arrangements (Veggeland 2009).

It is difficult, however, to change conflicting legal regulations and contracts because the courts effect such changes. These changes are therefore not effected by politicians, corporatist institutions, or trade unions. The relations between the unions of interest groups and the state arose during the twentieth century, these relations in Scandinavia being in accordance with traditions of consensual policy-making (see Chap. 5). The role of interest groups in policy-making has, however, weakened in recent decades. Privileged groups are no longer invited to important deliberations on public policies, only gaining access when decision-makers assess that the benefits will exceed the costs of closely involving interest groups. This development has consequences for democratic procedures. On the one hand, more involved social groups present a broader set of inputs to the administrative and political process of decision-making. On the other hand, the price is a less transparent process of policy-making and a dependence on often hidden but legal steering agreements that are typical of the regulatory state.

Prevailing Governance Strategies of the Regulatory State

It has become commonplace to state that we live in the age of the regulatory state, this regime featuring the following: (1) *regulation* through modernization of public sector activity (Pollitt and Bouckaert 2004: 188–196); (2) *agencification* through the establishment of the "unelected" (Vibert 2007) arm's-length agencies and regulatory bodies and authorities[5]; (3) *transformation of institutional self-regulation from internal to external*; and (4) *formalization of relationships* within policy domains, through legal agreements and contract-based relationships.

The Strategy of Modernization

Modernization is perhaps the most obvious cause of the regulatory boom (Moran 2001). According to Pollitt and Bouckaert (2004), the policy of privatization as a part of the strategy of modernization has led to the trend of minimizing the public administrative apparatus. This involves the handing over of as many tasks as possible directly to the market sector through privatization and indirectly through contracting out, through outsourcing. It has been called the "hollowing out" of the state apparatus, a social-institutional arrangement in which social security and public services of all kinds, including social and health services, telecommunications, electricity, railways, energy, and even military services, are drastically reduced. The privatization of essential infrastructural services is significant given that these sectors have been widely viewed as an essential component of the modern state's responsibility.

The ideas of Schumpeter were obvious and evident in this privatization strategy: to spur economic growth by reducing the rigid state machine through a minimizing strategy and to replace it with innovative market actors that compete and become winners, so causing the closing down of old industries that are according to Schumpeter (1942/1979), exposed to "creative destruction." The market winners generated by competition remain under regulatory control. Such actors intensify the direct contact and relations between the political system and the market economy, unmediated by what is looked upon as rigid Weberian bureaucratic structures. State minimalists categorically reject the idea that governments should be put into a central position in the polity, to act in the best interest of the economy and the public social sphere. In Schumpeter's world, governments are considered "able" because they win votes, not because they have governed or will govern well (Kuper 2004: 98). State minimalists also use the measurements and mechanisms calibrated for the regulatory state, minimizing strategy accompanied by policies for tax cuts and low

---

[5]Other notions used in the same frameworks and with the same defined meanings are "non-majoritarian institutions" (Moran 2003), "distributed governance bodies" (OECD 2002), and "executives" (Christensen and Lægreid 2006).

interest rates that target an increase in aggregated consumption and investment followed by private-law regulations. The minimizing strategy represents, in total, the political economy of the regulatory state (Veggeland 2009).

The marketizing of the administrative system was an alternative strategy for instituting as many market-type mechanisms (MTMs) as possible within the public sector. This marketizing strategy implies not only a redefinition of the economic rules of the state, but also a transformed perspective on governments and their roles as regulatory authorities.

The marketizing strategy of New Public Management (NPM) essentially created the so-called public-law agencies (PLAs) and private-law bodies (PLBs). According to the OECD, these society processes are steered indirectly by law, regulation, and financial means (OECD 2002). They have acquired, in a democratic framework, the label of "unelected bodies," i.e., non-parliamentary arm's-length bodies (Vibert 2007). There is an emphasis on the achievement of results through the means of flexible organizational structures and competition.

This approach dovetails with Schumpeter's idea that innovation only becomes beneficial through competition in markets corrected for externalities. Public sector organizations should therefore, similarly, be made flexible and competitive but under the supervision of law, management by objectives, and regulations. This would increase efficiency and encourage users to value the individual freedom to choose.

Marketizing strategy, like the state minimizing strategy, prepared the way for the policies of tax cuts and low interest rates that were supposed to effect an increase in aggregated consumption and investment and thereby economic growth. Marketizing strategy has turned out to be characteristic of the government of the regulatory state, namely, "steering without rowing," steering at a distance from government and indirectly by law and regulation, as Majone (1997) tells us, not by parliamentary bodies, central planning, and public ownership. Administrations subscribing to NPM, especially in the Anglo-American tradition from the beginning of the 1980s, adopted this strategy extensively (Knill 2001; Veggeland 2007).

For the political economy, the aim of the modernization of the administrative system was to introduce faster, more flexible ways of budgeting, managing, and delivering services to users by applying regulatory measures. Unelected arm's-length bodies were organized and set into motion as market actors or pseudo-market actors. The predication was that the distinctiveness of public provision, that is, "services of general interest," inherited a necessity to distinguish between "noncommercial services," in-house services under Weberian bureaucratic protection and control, and "commercial services," marketized services under public or private-law supervision (EU green paper 2003).

Some have, broadly speaking, interpreted the arrival of the regulatory state in the form of instrumental governance to be an extension of the powers of the state, based on standardization through regulation, quantification, and considerable public reporting (Moran 2003). There was a need to strengthen the state innovatively through multilevel governance and through European integration and globalization rather than the dilution of the state and privatization. One example was the wave for reducing vertical differentiation and the creation of internal markets in the name of EU regulations that swept over local government.

The reduction of hierarchical levels in the municipalities tier unit created an organizational vacuum, NPM instruments and regulatory measurements, such as balanced scorecards, internal quasi-markets, value-based management, and steering by contracts, soon filling this vacuum. A comparative study of European local governments in this context is, however, lacking. A long row of research questions is to ask and require answers. A bottom-up perspective on the local impacts of the regulatory state ought to be brought up and forwarded to decision-makers by impact analyses. We would also ask the following questions. What are the costs of the local implementation of EU regulations and national regulations? What are the similarities and differences between internal regulation after the administrative delayering of European and Scandinavian municipalities? What are the possible explanations of such similarities and differences in the framework of the regulatory state? Did the implementation of the delayered administration strengthen the local government, or did it instead dilute the steering capacity?

Strategy and Agencification

Agencification may be defined in terms of a large and growing world of "unelected" arm's-length agencies and regulatory bodies and authorities. Frank Vibert (2007: 5) presents this picture of the varied world of the "unelected": "Unelected bodies include central banks, independent risk management bodies, independent economies and ethics regulators, regimes of inspection and audit and new types of appeal bodies." As self-governing organizations, they are by law given the mandate and have the ability to borrow money, to earn money from financial investments, to hire and employ staff, to contract service suppliers, and to manage their resources. Regulatory state governments have sought to apply a more marketized approach by organizing these as unelected competitive stakeholders. The transformation toward "businesses" remains, however, limited in the light of the framework of what the EU defines as providers of "services of general interest," noncommercial public services such as health, education, and the police.

In the context of external self-regulation, the "unelected" implies at least six aspects.

- The strategy of marketizing public services results in institutional agencification. A steering board, guided by law and regulations, is given autonomy in the governance of each agency.
- In the regulatory state, a "clean" audit and control are laid in the hands of a wide range of competing regulatory agencies, the implementation of commercial budget arrangements being forced (see Chap. 8).
- Frank Vibert (2007) portrays the "unelected" regulatory bodies as sharing democratic powers with the democratically elected representatives. He rejects the

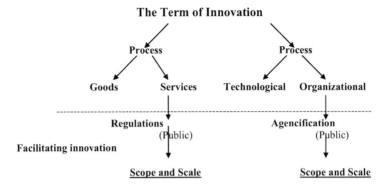

Fig. 3.1 Innovation in the regulatory state: a new perspective

view that unelected agency regimes are manifestations of increasing "democratic deficit." Vibert indeed concludes that the processes of agencification strengthen the democracy of the state, because of the sharing of state power. This conclusion may be valid under certain circumstances and within a particular perspective. It is, however, otherwise not because of the rise of the unelected as a universal concept entails the grave fragmentation and the abdication of representative democracy.

- Regulatory agencies as unelected and independent, non-majority parts of the state obviously constitute a reallocation of power bound to the innovative processes of agencification, as illustrated in Fig. 3.1. However, these processes have deep consequences for traditional liberal democracy, given the increased dominance of non-majority politics (Lodge 2007).
- There is a dilemma in finding a balance between non-majority and majority politics. The democratic legitimacy of "the regulatory state" relies on the state not distributing excessive regulatory authority to non-state bodies (OECD 2002). If this happens, then the state suffers from democratic deficit, almost per definition. Otherwise put, Vibert's perspective is too narrow.
- A judgment of whether or not agencification strengthens or dilutes democracy and good governance demands criteria which we can use to assess success or failure. We need criteria to be able to evaluate whether the innovation of regulatory bodies has led to successes or fiascos. Yet, this issue is all too rarely tackled (Black 2005). There is a need to formulate the criteria that can help us analyze the impacts of the regulatory state both in macro (globally) and in micro (locally).

Transformation of Institutional Self-Regulation

Universities were once self-regulated institutions, directed by a knowledge-based channel of professors with an elected rector, first among equals, and a consensus-based, representative university council. This communicative regime was in command. The autonomy and power of the elected regime had, however, its limitations.

It was internally under the budgetary control of an administration led by a managing director. This meant that, except for bureaucratic surveillance, control of the budget, and the implementation of national laws and the rules of the university sector, the rector and the other elected organs controlled this regime almost completely. The old regime of the university is, in principle, an example of traditional internal self-regulation of highly profiled professional institutions that also includes medical and numerous other institutions, which have now been transformed. It is important to note that the university is an example "in principle," because although the institutional structure could be organized in various ways, it always had the characteristic of a leadership rooted in the profession of scholars, belonging to the actual institution which provides the service, or the professions of experts monitoring themselves. The key characteristic of internal traditional self-regulation is therefore the right and duty of the institution to independently establish its own regulatory standards and methods of consensus. This form of self-regulation has greatly declined.

The transformation of self-regulation represents a new face of the regulatory state that is very important but rarely noticed: reconstruction to steering instruments (Moran 2003: 93). Why have so few recognized that old integrated internal hierarchies of public service have been modified in favor of much more loosely coordinated organizations of public agencies and bodies? One reason may very well be that scholars and researchers of academic institutions tend to be adverse to regulatory measures. This group is viscerally "anti-regulatory" according to Roger King (2007: 151) that is "regulatory scholarship for higher education researchers is regarded as either empirically inapplicable or normatively suspect." The breakdown of internal hierarchies and control was implemented, replacing these with external controls and external boards that included all kinds of professionals nominated by the government. Acting as professional board members, these professionals often participate in diverse public service institutions and possess skills that are normally different from those of the internal professionals. The aim is to have top-paid, professional managing directors who possess the one supposed skill of professional management: the general leading and controlling of the internal professionals.

The notion of transformed self-regulation in Anglo-Saxon states and in states heavily influenced by this administrative tradition tends to indicate certain ideological overtones. This includes independence from the hierarchy, facilitation of local empowerment, more efficiency, reduced power of trade unions, the inclusion of interest groups, and equality under the "law" (as outlined in Chaps. 5 and 6). This tradition, however, often overlooks the fact that the state plays a large directing role, albeit a regulatory one, by establishing for example economic incentives, rules, surveillance, and budgets bound to output and results.

The institutions, after the transformation, follow the idea of management by objectives. The government sets the objectives, decides the regulatory framework, and allocates financial means in accordance with reported achievements and regulation. There are, apart from this, no interventions. Proclamations of enlarged and decentralized institutional autonomy are therefore made under the umbrella of the board's decision-making. Profession-based, self-regulating service-providing institutions have become what some have termed "formal organizations" (Røvik 2007).

"Formal organization" indicates an understanding of organizations as being basically universal and similar in structure, in terms of command and control mechanisms. This term therefore implies that management is a universal skill applicable to any professional service, regardless of the substance of the provision and the particular professional skill needed to secure quality and the innovation of processes and offers.

The trend of managing by objectives, that is, the management of formal organizations and governance by contracts, besides transforming the concept of self-regulation also takes power away from the trade unions and other interest groups. This feature is specifically pronounced in Anglo-Saxon states, but it also appears in other countries where the regulatory state rules. This chapter describes a Scandinavian approach to the issue of trade union power. The Scandinavian countries have traditionally scored high on the different measures for the presence of strong trade unions and their involvement, in short, corporatism. Corporatism is one of the institutions that enhance consensual policy-making. However, as we have noted, traditional corporatist structures are, for several reasons, under erosion. The current inclusion of interest groups in policy-making bodies is much less comparable to the heyday of corporatism in the 1970s, the inclusion of interest groups in policy-implementing bodies varying greatly. Chapter 5 concludes that while they are still strong in Denmark, they have been strongly reduced in Norway, Sweden being somewhere in the middle. The question is whether and to what extent this development is a sign of the withering away of consensual politics or whether it is only a sign of greater flexibility in the way political and bureaucratic actors interfere with strong interest groups. Answers derived from this comparative analysis highlight the self-regulatory concept.

The strong attachment of the people, politicians, and scholars to the idea of self-regulation makes the idea extremely powerful across the Western democracies. As a consequence, it is common to hear the invocation of the traditional language of self-regulation to justify the institutional arrangements that currently characterize the regulatory state. We may not, however, in any sense or by any stretch of the imagination equate the term of "self-regulation" of today with the traditional term of self-regulation. The earlier use of the term refers to the regulatory state principle of "steering by rowing," while the new use refers to the opposite principle of "steering without rowing." These principles are contextually defined and must be used accordingly.

Few self-regulatory agreements are immune to change, nor was the earlier, internal, professional self-regulation of higher education and university research. The reorganization of this self-regulatory system of state funding of research was launched and executed over the last 10 years, the Nordic countries also becoming involved in this process of innovation. In Norway, a substantial change to the self-regulatory model of incentives for scientific publishing did not come into force until 2006. The rules of the model set requirements for the inclusion of publications and the extra scores given to publications of high quality. The rules, not professional referees, decide (Gabrielsen et al. 2007).

Formalization of Relationships

The formalization of relationships within the domains of regulated policy is a notion that entails legal agreements and contract-based relationships. This notion suggests that deliberative discourses and discretionary powers have been reduced in the current multilevel system of governance.

The reduction of discretionary powers has been partly due to the importance of European law and rules and their penetration of local and national levels without deliberation and without implementation being decided by elected assemblies. This is partly due to the role of new public management and the processes of agencification, which create unelected regulatory agencies. It is also partly due to the trend of formalizing relationships in the public sector as public–public or public–private partnerships, or of contracting out the provision of public services. Formal laws and rules are closely bound to the regulatory state order. So are partnership formations and legal contract-based governance.

The Study of Regulatory Innovation

The study of regulation[6] in the broad field of politics has therefore concentrated on four interrelated policy choices (Lodge 2003). Lodge promotes the prevailing of privatization of services, which public institutions and organizations formerly provided, the emergence of self-regulatory unelected agencies, which also have quasi-legislative power for economic regulation of marketized activities, and the formalization of relationships such as contract-based partnerships within a particular policy domain. Linked to the marketizing and formalization choices has been the growing use of outsourcing of public service provisions, for example, public tendering procedures. The growing presence and importance of EU legislation are significant in these interrelated fields. Studies of the supranational level of the EU and corresponding national levels of analysis have therefore focused on the organizational forms of the regulatory state (arm's-length agencies and bodies, including partnerships), or processes of multilevel governance and regulatory change and innovation (Kjær 2004). The studies also concentrate on selective sectoral approaches that have the goal of taming the "risk society" (Beck 1992; Veggeland 2009). The long list of global cases of risk includes economic, social, and ethnic problems and environmental problems such as ethics and challenges to bad governance (Rothstein and Torell 2005).

---

[6]The idea of "regulation" as a political process is arguably rooted in its etymology. The term "regulation" is rooted in the Latin "regulare" (to control by rule) and appears in the English language just before the Westphalian Treaty of 1648. By 1715, "regulation" was defined as "rule for management." A regulator was established as a member of a commission or board to manage governance.

According to Charles Edquist,[7] innovation in its broadest sense was traditionally viewed as being a consequence of processes that lead to new goods, new technologies, organizational change, or new private service provisions—all products that are successful in the market; see Fig. 3.1. The public sector and its actors of infrastructure and service providers were not part of this production order, because of being organized beyond market competition and driven by political objectives and budgetary allocations. Central planning and predictive bureaucratic administration ought not to give any room to innovative actions. However, the public sector has moved far from the Weberian ideal of bureaucracy in the contemporary modernized society and has been brought in line with the principles of NPM (Kjær 2004). This transformation into hybrid and self-regulatory organizations results in new conditions for innovation and for innovative activity in the public sector, for the production of services and the processes leading up to them.

LSE Public Policy Group, UK, (2008: 6), for example, expands this trend and talks about innovations as new ideas which are: "New to world/UK, New to public sector/voluntary sector, New to region/locality, New to this government organization." The arrival of the regulatory state has furthermore expanded the perspective on regulation. Regulation has come to mean a new sort of necessary societal service, a kind of product of public governance and steering. Studies have made it clear that each regulation is best understood as an impetus for an unspecified range of new regulations: in other words, "hyper"-regulatory innovations for the sake of realizing the original one, with explanatory references to spillover processes (Moran 2001). The growing number of regulations to be adopted and executed also means we also see the introduction of the new regulatory agencies and bodies, that is, agencification as organizational innovation.

The EU is a good example. The EU's regulatory and monetary measure system is closely linked to European agencies and bodies and plays a legal role in the economic and social domains of its member states. At the national level, regulation is followed up by bodies responsible for implementation, thereafter by agencies responsible for surveillance and control. These also represent organizational innovations. According to Black et al. (2005), "regulatory innovation" is part of the extended terms of references in the framework of innovation in the private and public domains. Figure 3.1 illustrates this broad perspective on innovation.

Figure 3.1 indicates that regulation in the regulatory state represents a type of service making through scope and scale, markets, institutions, and communities functioning. Regulation is understood to be the deliberate and sustained attempt to change the behavior of others toward standards and goals that are mostly produced by public sector actors, but processed by agencies and other governmental bodies. The proposed innovation model focuses on regulation that facilitates innovation and may fit with state activities involved in processes of regulatory delivery and processes of making contracts between actors, for example, partnership contracts. However, this needs adjustment to apply regulations in a wider sense. We have

---

[7]Lecture held at Lillehammer University College, Norway, January 28, 2009.

already drawn attention to five explanatory conceptions of regulation that point to five key areas benefiting from regulatory services. These are regulations (1) as authoritative rules, (2) as efforts of state agencies to manage the economy, (3) as mechanisms of steering and performing legal control, (4) as extensions of multilevel governance and network coordination, and (5) as means and measures to handle environmental threats and the "risk society of the new modernity" (Beck 1992). To sum up, we are talking about innovations in regulatory processes, in risk identification and reduction, and in risk analysis and management (Sparrow 2000). It is fully feasible to study the intensity and inclination of innovation in this context. Studies focused on the scope and scale of newly implemented regulations may quite effectively indicate the degree of innovative ability and performance of the three listed fields or aspects of state governance and areas of responsibility (Veggeland 2007).

Agencification performance, Fig. 3.1, is a key element of the regulatory state order. Our presentation of four characteristics of this order included the marketizing of public sector services. Marketizing relates closely to the other characteristics, that is, the establishment of "unelected" arm's-length agencies and regulatory bodies, the transformation of institutional self-regulation into external control, and the formalization of relationships within policy domains, embodied as institutionalizing agreements and contract-based relationships. We can label these collectively as parts of the processes of "agencification," illustrated in Fig. 3.1. The study of innovation of the regulatory state in this respect focuses on processes favoring new scopes and scales for not only public surveillance and control but also service provision and management linked to agencies. There is therefore a concentration on legal European and national acts and institutional changes and reforms within the framework of regulatory governance and goal achievement. The ability to innovate in the public sector is measurable by its political acceptance and functionality, and innovative frequency gives an indication of innovative intensity (Mørth 2004).

Innovation of Institutions and Regulations

If we define all innovation simply as change, then we must conclude that all changes are innovative. This definition, however, is unsatisfactory and leads to an equally unsatisfactory conclusion. This lack of precision has inspired studies on the criteria of change and innovation. One aspect relates to the distinction between subjectivity and objectivity. An innovation may be experienced at the individual and personal level as being subjective change. An individual changes his or her work routine to that stipulated in a given labor regulation and adjusts to it in a way that best suits his or her day-to-day life. The regulation may not be an innovation and instead one adopted by diffusion from somewhere else. The personal experience of this might, however, be of this being an innovation. In contrast, from a perspective of governance, there is a greater focus on the fact that innovation is an objective experience that can be empirically measured as a significant change of progress. Researchers can identify laws and regulations that introduce new work routines for environmental treatment, improvement of productivity or hospital care, for example, and conveniently count them as technological innovations (Black et al. 2005).

The concept of innovation differs from the concept of invention. Innovation, both subjective and objective, differs from policy inventions or ideas that have not been implemented (Rogers 2003). Innovation is characterized by the effort to rejuvenate and the presence of benevolent motives. In this view, regulations are service goods produced to help stabilize society and to counteract risks or to offer another way of organizing society by agencifications, namely, unelected agencies and other arm's-length bodies (see Fig. 3.1). Hence, regulatory innovations have two faces.

In the regulatory state, institutional innovations are part of the organizational changes of processes, as indicated by Fig. 3.1. Innovation in institutional structures and organizational processes includes the creation of new organizations in the form of agencies and the innovation of regulatory services when the norms, rules, and standards of operating procedures undergo change. In simple terms, innovation denotes the use of new solutions for old problems, or of old solutions to address "new" problems. Generally, innovation is a facet of the modernist project of rationalization, systematization, and ordering.

Regulatory innovations take place in different contexts, such as different administrative traditions and models such as the Anglo-Saxon, Continental, and Scandinavian or Nordic traditions (Knill 2001; Veggeland 2007). Innovation can be measured in the context of a geographical area (state, region, or municipality), a policy domain (welfare, social, and physical environment), some other unit of analysis (organizational or individual), or a mixture of different regulatory approaches. The mixture approach could be a study of the economic regulations in the EU, social regulations in Scandinavia, or environmental regulations in the Arctic region.

Regulatory Innovation: A Case of Scandinavian Involvement with the EU

The diffusion of EU laws and regulations impinges on national states that are under the dominance of this supranational, multilevel regime of governance. The way in which member states pronounce, translate, and implement these regulations and what may be the best way to do so have been issues of great concern. Such questions demand a historical consideration of each state's administrative tradition and welfare state model (Knill 2001; Iversen 2005; Veggeland 2007). In our context, we may propose two theses (Røvik 2007).

(A) The copying or imitation thesis: When a state adapts and implements a regulatory act, for example, a European Union directive, the state may very well take the act literally, each member state imitating and copying the style of implementation from others, most often from the most dominant states and ideologies within the Community. Such copying activities do not lead to regulatory innovation.

(B) The innovation thesis: The public authorities of a member state that administer the legal aspects and the implementation of European Union regulations recognize their own administrative traditions. Hence, their translation aims to adjust these through reformulations, that is, re-regulations. They do so to achieve national or local political objectives in a legally sound manner. We can name this practice modernization by regulatory innovations (Black et al. 2005).

Let us consider these theses more closely by examining a Scandinavian case. First, we describe an EU-adopted regulation on public procurement from the early 1990s. This regulation demanded that all public purchases that are not in-house provisions of goods and services over the marginal cost level of 200,000 Euros are required to be exposed to market competition through tendering and outsourcing. This exposure is to take the form of open or partly open tendering and bidding rounds and the contracting out of the provisions to the private providers who win each of the many rounds.

Next, we must account briefly for the background. We focus here on the EEA negotiations at the beginning of 1990 between EFTA countries and the EU on an agreement for access to the EU single market. The countries in question entered into the EEA agreement. Sweden, then an EFTA country, however, instead became an EU member in 1994, Norway continuing as an EEA country. The EEA agreement included the EU's supranational set of rules and directives on the public purchasing of products and services. Procedures which at that time used a threshold of 200,000 Euros (1,600,000 Norwegian krone (NOK)) were established for such purchases. Purchases for lower values did not require competition and bidding. Norway was, moreover and in order to ensure compliance, placed under the EFTA Surveillance Agency (ESA).

As with many other EU member states, there were substantial obstacles and skeptical attitudes toward the introduction of outsourcing in the public sector in Scandinavian societies (Veggeland 2004). This reticence was due to path dependency and popular and social-democratic concerns about private sector involvement in traditional public activities. The other concern was related to very few services not being liable to outsourcing, from the Scandinavian perspective of a universal welfare state and furthermore despite the great technical variety. The lack of clarity on which "services of general interest"[8] (EU Green paper 2003) ought to remain in-house provisions and which should be exposed to competition became defined as an attack on the universal welfare state. The challenge to existing public service provision also triggered resistance from public employees and unions affected by this and their political allies. Finally, some perceived the outsourcing game as one where private

---

[8]The EU defines the term "services of general interest" as public services which the government provides and ought to provide under universal obligation. The diversification of this type of services for in-house provision or outsourcing is still heavily disputed within the Union (see the dispute on the "service directive").

big businesses would come out as winners and consequently unbalance the Scandinavian mixed economy by enervating small and medium-sized businesses (SMBs) and harming local and regional economies.

This general skeptical attitude toward expanding the outsourcing concept and bringing it in line with the EU directive had considerable implications. The Scandinavian states introduced innovative re-regulation, which was influenced by the EEA agreement and also probably by the traditions of "small is beautiful" and the welfare state. Norway and Sweden set the dividing line for bidding much lower than the EU regime required, NOK 200,000[9] and SEK 200,000, respectively. The decision resulted in a much more extensive use of bidding and outsourcing than would have been the case if the EU's marginal value for public purchasing had been applied. The decision was legal because the EU directive had no restrictions on lower national limits for bidding and competition, and, the directive was therefore open to interpretation and translation (Veggeland 2005). Obviously, a high proportion of public purchases would exceed this amount owing to the relatively high level of prices and costs in the two Scandinavian countries.

Why, then, does this adaptation and this setting of a lower limit count as an example of regulatory innovation? It counts because the authorities in both countries recognized and adhered to their administrative traditions and models. This lends support to thesis B. Likewise, the authorities neither copied nor imitated the EU regulation of public procurements and the use of outsourcing, but made instead a decision of their own making—a re-regulation that points to innovation thesis B.

What was the result of this independent and innovative turn on outsourcing and of the two Scandinavian regulatory solutions in the wake of this specific Europeanization mode of institutional penetration? The innovation entailed both positive and negative impacts according to certain criteria. On the positive side, an incentive was created through the use of this particular outsourcing concept of public administration that encouraged SMBs to participate in the markets. Small providers with limited resources for investment gained the opportunity to participate and adjust their activities to compete for public procurement and tendering, due to the low regulatory cost. Numerous and flexible SMBs came out as winners in a large number of bidding rounds. In becoming contractors, they contributed to the significant creation of employment, and private and public services spread all over the two Scandinavian countries, thereby sustaining territorial and social balance in the states' mixed economies (Veggeland 2007). The negative side of this re-regulation gradually became apparent as rising transactional costs began to emerge. Transactional costs rose in the public sector due to the extensive administration that was required for each round of bidding, the evaluation of offers from the many providers, and the ensuing contracting and control procedures. Also, many providers assigned many resources in vain to tendering, as participation in the many bidding rounds would not always turn out successfully (Scharpf 1997; Veggeland 2004).

---

[9]In 2005, the amount was increased to NOK 500,000 by the government, now NOK 1100.

In short, these empirical facts from this Scandinavian example support thesis B of innovation: the regulatory public authorities in the two countries acted innovatively in relation to the EU's regulatory regime. It was a path-dependent, contextual innovation, and not an imitation.

Dilemmas of the Regulatory State

Regulatory state order is not only of interest as a subject for empirical exploration. It is also the source of significant dilemmas that highlight crucial issues affecting states globally. This section explores four dilemmas of the regulatory state that not only suggest reasons for instability and for policy and democratic deficits but also more fundamental dysfunctions.

The Dilemma of the Numerous Regulatory Agencies

The huge number of so-called public or semi-public "unelected" bodies (Vibert 2007) that wield power in the structures of modern democratic states comes often as a surprise to many. It should not, however, as the rise of such bodies is closely connected to the arrival of the regulatory state (OECD 2002). Different terminology is used to describe these bodies. Many are named "regulatory agencies," meaning that either they are regulated producers of services or they are legally empowered to be auditing and controlling agencies (Braithwaite 2008: 56). The intention of the international and national central authorities is in line with the regulatory state order of "governing without rowing." That is, not acting as executives but as regulators. The bodies can operate with different degrees of autonomy and also take different legal forms, depending on whether they are subject to public or private law, or "public-law agencies" (PLAs) or "private-law bodies" (PLBs), respectively (OECD 2002: 18–19).

This first dilemma emerges from the political element of the regulatory process. Governments are behind the granting of arm's-length autonomy, that is to say a certain distance from direct political interests and involvements. This arrangement is, however, at best a vulnerable construction. In the regulatory state, politicians decide goals and budgets. Granting regulatory bodies full authority over specific decisions and promises is, however, more or less an "abdication" in some fields. In exchange, politicians, however, benefit from proclaiming that they have offered the solution to a given problem to the constituents that benefit from the regulatory regime. The dilemma is connected to the division of responsibility. If something goes wrong, who is to blame? Is it the government or the arm's-length body? In the regulatory state, one idiom of politics seems ubiquitous—"the politics of blame avoidance" (Weaver 1986). The sharing of authority and responsibility makes the primary interest of both shareholders the avoidance of blame. Politicians tend to take both the responsibility and the honor of regulatory successes, but disavow the regime when failures occur. Consequently, the unelected bodies blame the government for bad budgetary balances, excessively narrow regulatory frameworks, and duplicity when success fails to materialize. Bargaining processes then stagnate, so reducing the innovative capacity of the public domain.

Public–private partnerships and the hybrid form of public–public partnership[10] furthermore count as regulatory agencies. In the regulatory state, partnerships are established as institutional instruments aimed at mobilizing and facilitating activity in multi-actor and multilevel settings. "End-means" thinking dominates the notion of partnership, aspects that are quite obvious in regional politics and in planning at the European level and the national level. Network contacts, negotiations, and bargaining launch target agreement and contract processes between public and private regional actors and multilevel administrations. The goal is that achievements are made feasible through cooperation and increased steering capacity, the steering capacity being embedded in the agreements. The sharing of authority and responsibility means that the shareholders are interested in cooperation rather than competition, the concept of regional partnerships being the government's preferred policy for extending territorial competition within the regulatory state.

The dilemma here is that judicial agreement-based governance and regulatory mechanisms move the direction from traditional democratic governance, which derives its legitimacy from the representative decision-making of the elected, to a model where legitimacy depends on the partnership's capacity to accomplish goals and achieve results. In short, legitimacy becomes a legitimacy of output (Veggeland 2003). There are two conflicting regimes, and a balance between them is hard to strike. But there is no doubt that the regulatory state has a bias for the output model. The friction between the two may, even so, disrupt settled agreements and decrease innovative capacity at the regional and local levels.

The Dilemma of Hyper-regulation Leading to Hyper-innovation

Regulation in one sector or at one level of administration tends to generate new regulations as "spillover" in the neo-functionalist sense (Jensen Strøby 2004). The creation of regulatory measures and means generates further regulatory innovations. The dilemma, then, is that innovation tends to create hyper-innovation in the regulatory state. Michael Moran's thesis (2003: 26) is that innovation in institutional affairs has been a "fiasco" and has engendered more innovation in an ever ascending,

---

[10]The notion of public–public partnership actually indicates a hybrid organization even though it is all public, because public administrations and public service providers have been split up and made independent arm's-length bodies furnished with the legal authority to sign agreements and contracts.

or more accurately descending, spiral. He argues that the era in the United Kingdom of the last 30 or so years has been one of "hyper-innovation," "the frenetic selection of new institutional modes, and their equally frenetic replacement by alternatives" (Moran 2003: 26).

The consequences of these trends are multiple. One is the growing lack of transparency of regulatory administrations due to the number of regulations and innovations and the frequency of institutional changes. Holistic approaches become lost and so do the possibilities of political coordination and steering ability. Rising transactional costs associated with fragmented administrative functions are a well-known repercussion (Scharpf 1997). We can observe in Scandinavia and the rest of Europe that the direction of reforms from the 1980s is toward more hierarchy, more formality, and more state control. "These observations can be reconciled with prevailing images of the regulatory state, but at tremendous intellectual cost," concludes Moran (2003: 9).

In the regulatory state, there seems to be a need for criteria to evaluate outcomes. As we have seen above, if we want to be able to determine whether or not regulatory innovations have led to "successes" or "fiascos," good or bad governance, a determination that is difficult to and too rarely carried out, then we need criteria against which we can make these assessments. The criteria might be formulated as standards, social rights, or ethical norms and values (Veggeland 2009). The last chapter of this book presents an example of research that critically analyzes such criteria with reference to international investment funds.

The Dilemma of Exponential Rise of Transactional Costs

An OECD report from 2002 (2002: 21–26) drew conclusions about the dilemmas associated with the regulatory state. Another report, "Modernising Government: the way forward" (OECD 2005) analyzed these further. These reports have raised the following points.

- In most countries, and in line with the new democratic principles, priorities have moved away from the inclination to create new independent and separate bodies. Now the challenge seems to be finding the right balance between accountability, autonomy, and management of the existing independent agencies and bodies through more openness and transparency, and through strengthening the steering capacity of governments.
- The new unelected technocratic entities allow governments to avoid taking political decisions or to take decisions guided only by technical expertise on issues that require a political choice and that are at the core of political responsibility.
- The lack of clarity about the differences between the various types of agencies, authorities, and corporations makes it unclear whether the best organizational

forms have been chosen for the purposes of government. Standardizing measures have instead been implemented.

- Governmental monitoring efforts and control of the independent public entities are becoming more difficult. Despite the presence of reporting procedures and of neutral agencies for legal surveillance, the different types of relationships and mechanisms of control and accountability make accurate control almost impossible.
- The lack of clarity of the institutional system potentially undermines citizens' trust in the systems' functions.
- There is an acknowledgement of the need for clearer criteria for establishing different types of boards—advisory, management or governing boards, and their respective responsibilities. There has been criticism of the lack of transparency surrounding the appointments of board members, their salaries, and other benefits. Other criticisms have focused on the lack of representative status of the members with respect to gender, ethnic, and local background.
- The independent bodies are seen as functioning outside political debate, functioning with little oversight of ministers and ministries, and as having weak arrangements for accountability. Parliaments are neglected, and so are individuals and institutions of civil society. The conclusion is that weak mechanisms of accountability undermine the legitimacy of governments and parliaments.
- Finally, weak mechanisms of coordination and failures of coherence threaten effective public service production and the achievement of "best value" for individuals, social groups, and corporate interests due to fragmented governance.

With regard to the last point on weak coordinating mechanisms, we can refer to what has been called Scharpf's Law (Hooghe and Marks (2001: 5)): "As the number of affected parties increases . . ... negotiated solutions incur exponentially rising and eventually prohibitive transaction costs" (Scharpf 1997: 70).

According to this law, the problems of technical, communicative, or legal coordination in the regulatory state system are associated with the number of actors and bodies involved and escalate immensely as numbers grow. Transactional costs will also ultimately be prohibitive. Scharpf's Law insists that the weak coordinating mechanisms of the reporting countries are not evidence of poor performance of public governance, but actually a *consequence* of the regulatory state itself, because of its inclination to spur hyper-regulation and hyper-innovation (Veggeland 2009).

Therefore, according to the earlier of the two OECD reports (2002), there is a growing focus on *good governance and more coherent public services*, that is, on solutions of policy and structural coherence, including ensuring that the autonomous bodies collaborate on joint projects and in public–public partnerships. The focus of the states in the study is furthermore reported to be on the following endeavors: (a) the attempt to avoid the creation of new independent agencies, public service enterprises, and autonomous bodies; (b) the increased involvement of civil society and governments in governance; (c) the improvement of parliamentary control over activities to achieve more holistic responsibility; and finally, (d) the recognition of a growing political will to make the overall system more legible and accessible to citizens, and the accountability mechanisms, activities, and performance more easily controllable by parliaments at all tiers and in accordance with the principle of subsidiarity.

The European Union seems to now be taking this last principle seriously. According to the EU, decision-making in all fields in the Union should be at the lowest possible but effective level. The Treaty of Maastricht of 1993 introduced the principle of subsidiarity more as a political guideline than as a juridical norm, because of the elasticity of the formula. The new Treaty of Lisbon, whose ratification is expected in 2010, will transform subsidiarity into a hard regulation. This will mean that conflicts between member states and the Union on issues of competence may be brought to the European Court of Justice for solution. It is clear, then, that there is a political will to make the overall system of the future more transparent and more resistant to the development of more hierarchical structures.

The Dilemma of Democratic and Legitimacy Deficits

As we have seen, the unelected arm's-length public agencies and bodies in the regulatory state have become so pervasive that we take them for granted and rarely reflect on how they fit together and relate more broadly to the principles of demo-cratic government and good governance. Regulations and the regulatory state order have been widely utilized to apply frameworks taken from elsewhere and therefore have been used as "dependent variables." Such an approach sets the regulatory state as a dependent variable of the defined liberal representative democracy and its legitimacy. In this context, the regulatory state appears to suffer from a deficit of democracy and legitimacy: less government *by* the people, more government *for* the people (Scharpf 1999; Veggeland 2004). The regulatory state of the EU is such a case.

The elected European Parliament is still a politically weak governmental institu-tion and remote from the arenas where the most crucial decisions are taken. Even so, innumerable laws and regulations are decided every year and implemented in the EU member and associate EEA states. National governments have become instruments, subordinated to unelected regulatory bodies that implement regulations and which penetrate administrations from the national to the local levels. Contextually, the issue of democratic deficit appears as a reality and a given almost per definition, but in what sense?

As a general phenomenon of the regulatory state, democratic deficit implies that elected tier assemblies and governments are by status and institutionally have become politically weakened, while technocratic regulatory and executive authori-ties have gained more dominance (see follow-up in Chap. 4).

Accordingly, the weakening of representative political authorities creates a deficit of input democracy, accountability, and legitimacy—in short, a deficit of govern-ment *by* the people (Scharpf 1999). Regulatory governance for the people and legal partnership institutions are replacing representative government institutions. As

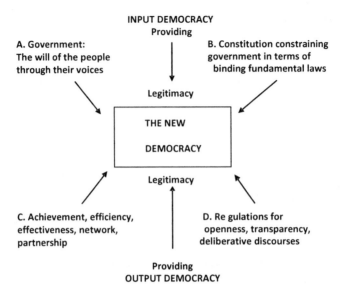

Fig. 3.2 Characteristics of the new democracy

Michael Keating (1998: 47) quipped, "governance is what exists when government is weak and fragmented," in the sense that unelected agencies and authorities are replacing more traditional governments with political holistic responsibilities.

In the regulatory state, policies gain their legitimacy first and foremost from achievements, efficiency, and effectiveness, that is, from the output or outcome of agencies and executives (Lane and Ersson 2003: 183–209). This output legitimacy challenges the traditional principles of parliamentary democracy and the liberal values of openness, transparency, and deliberative decision-making (Scharpf 1999; Veggeland 2004). Figure 3.2 illustrates some basic principles of both the input and output democratic orders (Veggeland 2003).

According to Fig. 3.2, the regulatory state constitutes both dependent and independent variables. The side of input democracy and the constraints of the Constitution substantiate parliamentary democracy. However, the function and legitimacy of these input elements depend very much on the organization of the regulatory state. Keating's (1998) statement that governance is what exists when government is weak and fragmented indicates that regulatory governance challenges and threatens the input democratic order. The solution would therefore appear to involve the restoration of this order by the building of strong and less fragmented government. Politically, this strategy is feasible in the European multilevel system of agreement-based government. Supranational democratic institutions integrated with national parliamentary democracy would increase the legitimacy of the new double-sided democracy.

On the other hand, the European regulatory state will continue to rely on an output democratic order, due to the new democratic order and as the bottom half of Fig. 3.2 shows. Hence, we must consider the output order in itself as being an independent variable, one which affects dependent variables such as achievements, efficiency, effectiveness, networks, and partnerships. However, this output or outcome democracy faces two threats. One from the unelected regulatory type of agencies and bodies and the other from their "locked-in" management that undermines the principles of openness, transparency, and deliberative discourse. In the new democracy, a strong political will is crucial to the securing and strengthening of these dependent variables.

There are obviously several reasons behind the deficit of input and output democracy described here. Generally, however, the deficit is linked to the "borderless" network-society syndrome, the processes of globalization, and the approach of multilevel governance characteristic of the regulatory states (Scharpf 1999; Veggeland 2009).

Regulation Through Ethics

Public innovation is a key part of the debate on "reinventing government" (Osborne and Gaebler 1993) and "rediscovering institutions" (March and Olsen 1989). National loan capital-driven economies, as some economists (e.g., Lordon 2003) predicted years ago, are in a state of disorder. A serious international financial crisis surfaced in 2008, initially triggered by the largely deficit-driven US economy. Worse, these developments have debilitated monetarist techniques to regulate the economy at the national level, because of the international interdependence of financial markets, capital movement, and free trade arrangements (Jordana and Levi-Faur 2004). What, then, will be the monetarists' measures or techniques? It is inconceivable to imagine the regulatory approach and the arm's-length agencies of the national states, which have proliferated in recent decades, will now begin to retreat. On the contrary, the best prediction is that regulatory state acts, backed by law, will grow in importance (Stiglitz 2009). Furthermore, a transformation of national regulatory measures into global ones, which seemingly is a necessary response to this particular crisis, would not be surprising. Innovation in the form of supranational regulation of financial policy could start with international negotiations and agreements that lead to new agencies and a swarm of regulations, or the strengthening of old global agencies, as we see happening today with the International Monetary Fund (IMF).

Can we suppose that such measures will tame the power of the European regulatory state that currently is in trouble because of the lack of both output and input legitimacy? UK Brexit is a bad sign for the Union. Frédéric Lordon, economist and author, provides this characteristic of the new crisis: *Et la vertu sauvera le monde… Après la débâcle financière, le salut par l' "éthique" ?* [*And virtue is going to save the world….After the financial catastrophe, the salvation by "ethics"?*] (2003). He finds that the crisis is rooted in the techno-economic system of the regulatory state. He foreshadows, in his analysis, the current financial troubles and identifies the failures that triggered them. According to Lordon, there is a need for an ethical normative approach to tame and rescue the EU monetary and free market economics from a vast recession. There is much weight in the argument for the notion of ethics being viewed as part of economic policy and dynamics. This is true, even if it has mostly been overlooked in political economic theory.

Ethics was certainly neither a part of the Keynesian-investment and effective-demand policy nor part of the Schumpeterian, market-driven idea of "creative destruction" that spurs economic growth. However, in the thinking on revitalizing modes of welfare state economies since the 1970s, ethics in the sense of favoring social equality and security as a basic for good economic governance, along with the fight against corruption, has come into much greater focus (Veggeland 2009; Iversen 2005; Taylor-Gooby 2004).

In the petroleum-producing Scandinavian state of Norway, revenues from production are put into a fund for investment abroad. Ethics became a keyword for this investment. The Norwegian government took action to regulate its investment fund, which helps secure the future pensions of citizens, to avoid investment in industries that threaten sustainable development and the well-being of people in the country and region of investment. The Norwegian government established and developed the Norwegian petroleum industry by creating, in the 1970s, its own oil company, Statoil (now Equinor), and by giving attractive concessions and regulatory protection to the Norwegian supply industry. The government gained, through this, national control over the petroleum resources and the gigantic revenues in return.

Storting (the Norwegian Parliament) in 2004 adopted regulatory ethical guidelines to help ensure the integrity of the investments of the "Government Petroleum Fund." Two years later, the government renamed this fund the "Government Pension Fund—Global," to reflect a social-institutional change guided by ethical intentions. Government policy and structures gradually changed as the industry matured and the conditions of the markets, i.e., petroleum policies, and technologies, changed (Austvik 2003). The need for sustainability, ethics, and ecological protection became a fundamental globally agreed unloosening of government support.

The Norwegian petroleum sector now consists of more companies that have the ability to compete at the international scale. The state plays a more regulative role, but remains the main rent collector and capitalist in this sector. The government further addresses the role of the petroleum fund and considers the negative consequences that might have resulted if the Norwegian petroleum resources had been founded under the more liberal international economic regime of today. Moreover, how Norway's integration with the EU has affected the country's steering capacity and how EU obligations may affect ethical policy thinking are also discussed.

The primary objective of the fund's ethical guidelines is still to ensure that current and future generations in Norway will benefit from good returns from the fund. The government thus channels the return yielded by the fund into the state budget to cover state debt. The government will continue to do this for the foreseeable future. The upper limit for annual use in the real economy is the entire return, the return per year shown to be on average three percent of average revenue. The Norwegian Minister of Finance has called this a policy-ethical "generational solidarity."

Ethically, this "solidarity" expresses the government's wish to avoid encumbering the owners, that is, the citizens, with debt. Ideally, the current generation and future generations in Norway will be free of debt as a result of this strategy. For the many nations currently in a deep debt crisis, being free from debt is in itself an almost unachievable privilege.

International commentators have stated that the fund's ethical dimensions represent the gold standard among major institutional investment funds around the world (Time 2008). The government has identified itself with this lofty aim on several occasions. The Report to the Storting, No. 16 (2006–2007), confidently states that "the fund shall be the best in the world." The Ministry of Foreign Affairs insists that Norway has become a world leader in taking ethical considerations into the management of the Norwegian Government Pension Fund. This is a political statement that is not easy to follow up in a world where complex economic interests rule. Only future research can judge this, and only after criteria have been formulated and international conventions have agreed what is good governance and sustained regulatory approaches. Only then can a conclusion on the Norwegian ethical regulatory approach be drawn. What we know in our context is that the regulatory approach is innovatively based on both effective hard and soft regulation.

A main research question therefore is to estimate the role and impact of the hard and soft regulatory instruments used to facilitate ethical trade and the functioning of markets, in European integration. It is of interest to examine the regulation of relations between the EU member states, including Scandinavian countries such as Norway, and to illustrate governance structures by mirroring the regulatory state functions. Our impact analysis of the results takes into consideration the characteristics of different developed economies in Europe and different historical administrative traditions. More specifically, we ask:

- What characterizes the regulatory cooperation between the EU and the Scandinavian countries, particularly with respect to the hard and soft regulatory instruments employed to create greater compatibility between regulatory systems and to facilitate European integration?
- What mechanisms are at play within the EU-Scandinavian regulatory cooperation and how effective are these as regulatory instruments as ways to facilitate the Scandinavian universal welfare state model?

This chapter explores the development regulatory relations between the EU and Scandinavia, with an emphasis on the use of soft regulatory instruments within their social politics framework. The role of soft regulatory instruments in this case offers a useful contrast to the role of hard regulatory instruments.

The next chapter furthermore assesses the effectiveness of universal welfare state principles in the facilitation of good governance. Scandinavia includes the group of countries of Sweden, Finland, Denmark (full EU members), and Norway and Iceland (EEA members). This group has developed good governance that is anchored in what is called the Keynesian Social Democratic Welfare State Model.

The basic idea of the Social Democratic Model was that everyone benefits from the welfare state, individuals and businesses alike, and that all are dependent on the welfare state and will therefore presumably feel obliged to pay the state for running it. As we shall see, and in contrast to the neoliberal regulatory state, the idea is to socialize the cost of collective social security and support the capacity for individual independence from the always unstable market forces. The model was based on a Keynesian economy and the combination of high growth rate with full employment. The huge cost of maintaining a universal welfare system put pressure on the state to reduce social problems and increase revenue income. Some of the vital conditional settings seemed, however, to fail from the 1970s onward. The EC, now the EU, framed a pressure on the Keynesian economy, which was followed by regulations that promote more market and less state. The regulatory state was knocking on the Scandinavian welfare state door.

Our impact analysis is intended to be a specific contribution on Scandinavia and to the understanding of ongoing administrative reforms and governance (as a term) in contrast to elected government structures. Analysis of contemporary welfare states has predominantly paid attention to government intervention of public administration to provide protection and social security to the citizens.

What, however, about the Scandinavian countries? We focus in the next chapter on threats to the universal welfare state and contextually on the role of management by objectives, arm's-length bodies, and the dilemmas these reveal. The following chapter also provides an introduction to the use of NPM, its role in regulatory governance in the Scandinavian administrative setting, and the widening of the perspective of Scandinavia in Europe, one that is tightly linked to the supranational EU's regulatory type of governance outlined above.

References

Amdam, J., & Veggeland, N. (1998). *Teorier om samfunnsplanlegging [Theories on social planning]*. Oslo: Universitetsforlaget.

Austvik, O. A. (2003). *Norwegian natural gas: Liberalization of the European gas market*. Oslo: Europa-programmet.

Baldwin, R., & Cave, M. (1999). *Understanding regulation: Theory, strategy, and practice*. Oxford: Oxford University Press.

Baldwin, R., Scott, C., & Hood, C. (Eds.). (1998). *A reader on regulation*. Oxford: Oxford University Press.

Beck, U. (1992). *Risk society: Towards a new modernity*. London: Sage.

Black, J. (2005). What is regulatory innovation? In J. Black, M. Lodge, & M. Thatcher (Eds.), *Regulatory innovation: A comparative analysis*. Cheltenham, UK: Edward Elgar.

Black, J., Lodge, M., & Thatcher, M. (Eds.). (2005). *Regulatory innovation: A comparative analysis*. Cheltenham, UK: Edward Elgar.

Braithwaite, J. (2008). *Regulatory capitalism: How it works, ideas for making it work better*. Cheltenham, UK: Edward Elgar.

Cass, D. (2005). *The constitutionalization of the World Trade Organization: Legitimacy, democracy and community in the international trading system*. Oxford: Oxford University Press.

Castells, M. (1996). *The rise of the network society*. Oxford: Blackwell.

Christensen, T., & Lægreid, P. (Eds.). (2006). *Autonomy and regulations: Coping with agencies in the modern state*. Cheltenham, UK: Edward Elgar.

EU green paper. (2003). *Services of general interest*. Brussels: COM (2003) 270 European Commission.

Gabrielsen, T. S., Kaarbøe, O., Lommerud, K. E., Risa, A. E., & Vagstad, S. (2007). *Finansieringssystemet for universitets- og høyskolesektoren—teoretiske vurderinger [The financial system for the university and college sector: Theoretical evaluations]*. Bergen: University of Bergen.

Habermas, J. (1987). *The theory of communicative action*. Cambridge: Polity Press.

Hood, C., Rothstein, H., & Baldwin, R. (2004). *The government of risk: Understanding risk regulation regimes*. Oxford: Oxford University Press.

Hooghe, L., & Marks, G. (2001). Types of multi-level governance. *European Integration Online Papers, 5* (11).

Iversen, T. (2005). *Capitalism, democracy and welfare*. Cambridge: Cambridge University Press.

Jensen Strøby, C. (2004). Neo-functionalism. In M. Cini (Ed.), *European Union politics* (pp. 80–93). Oxford: Oxford University Press.

Jordana, J., & Levi-Faur, D. (Eds.). (2004). *The politics of regulation: Institutions and regulatory reforms for the age of governance*. Cheltenham, UK: Edward Elgar.

Keating, M. (1998). *The new regionalism: Territorial restructuring and political change*. Cheltenham, UK: Edward Elgar.

King, R. (2007). *The regulatory state in an age of governance: Soft words and big sticks*. New York: Palgrave.

Kjær, A. M. (2004). *Governance*. Cambridge: Polity Press.

Knill, C. (2001). *The Europeanization of national administrations*. Cambridge: Cambridge University Press.

Kuper, A. (2004). *Democracy beyond borders: Justice and representation in global institutions*. Oxford: Oxford University Press.

Lane, J. E., & Ersson, S. (2003). *Democracy: A comparative approach*. London: Routledge.

Lodge, J. E. (2003). Institutional choice and policy transfer: Reforming British and German railway regulation. *Governance, 16*(2), 159–178.

Lodge, M. (2007). *Regulation in regulatory state and European politics*. www.aei.pitt.edu/7951/

Lordon, F. (2003). *Et la vertu sauvera le monde... Après la débâcle financière, le salut par l' " éthique "? [And virtue is going to save the world... .After the financial catastrophe, the salvation by "ethics"?]*. Paris: Raisons d'agir.

LSE Public Policy Group. (2008). *Innovation in government organizations and public sector agencies and public service NGOs: Draft working paper*. London: NESTA.

Majone, G. (1994). The rise of the regulatory state in Europe. *West European Politics, 17*(3), 77–101.

Majone, G. (1997). From the positive to the regulatory state: Causes and consequences of change in the mode of government. *Journal of Public Policy, 17*(3), 139–189.

March, J., & Olsen, J. P. (1989). *Rediscovering institutions: The organizational basis of politics*. New York: Free Press.

May, P. (2002). *Regulations and motivations: Hard versus soft regulatory paths*. Paper presented at the 2002 annual meeting of the American Political Science Association, Boston.

McGowan, F., & Wallace, H. (1996). Towards a European regulatory state. *Journal of European Public Policy, 3*(4), 560–576.

Moran, M. (2001). The rise of the regulatory state in Britain. *Parliamentary Affairs, 54*, 19–34.

Moran, M. (2003). *The British regulatory State: High modernism and hyper-innovation*. Oxford: Oxford University Press.

Mörth, U. (Ed.). (2004). *Soft law in governance and regulation: An interdisciplinary analysis*. Cheltenham, UK: Edward Elgar.

OECD. (2002). *Distributed public governance: Agencies, authorities and other government bodies*. Paris: OECD.

OECD. (2005). *Modernising government: The way forward*. Paris: OECD.

Osborne, D., & Gaebler, T. (1993). *Reinventing government*. New York: Plume.

Pedersen, T. H. (2009). *Fra kommunale forvaltninger til 'forvaltningsløse' kommuner [From municipal administration to 'administration-free' municipalities]*. Tromsø: Tromsø Universitet.

Pierre, J. (Ed.). (2001). *Debating governance: Authority, steering and democracy*. Oxford: Oxford University Press.

Pollack, M. A. (2005). Theorizing EU policy-making. In H. Wallace, W. Wallace, & M. A. Pollack (Eds.), *Policy-making in the European Union* (pp. 13–49). Oxford: Oxford University Press.

Pollitt, C., & Bouckaert, G. (2004). *Public management reform: A comparative analysis*. Oxford: Oxford University Press.

Power, M. (1997). *The audit society: Rituals of verification*. Oxford: Oxford University Press.

Rhodes, R. A. W. (1997). *Understanding governance*. Buckingham: Open University Press.

Rogers, E. M. (2003). *Diffusion of innovations* (5th ed.). New York: Free Press.

Rothstein, B., & Torell, J. (2005). *What quality of Government?* Paper presented to the Göteborg University Conference: Quality of Government.

Røvik, K. A. (2007). *Trender og translasjoner: Ideer som formet det 21. århundrets organisasjon [Trends and translations: Ideas that formed organizations of the twenty-first century]*. Oslo: Universitetsforlaget.

Scharpf, F. (1997). *Games real actors play: Actor-centred institutionalism in policy research*. Boulder, CO: Westview Press.

Scharpf, F. (1999). *Governing in Europe: Effective and democratic?* Oxford: Oxford University Press.

Schumpeter, J. A. (1942/1979). *Capitalism, socialism and democracy*. London: Allen & Unwin.

Selznick, P. (1985). Focusing organizational research on regulation. In R. Noll (Ed.), *Regulatory policy and the social sciences* (pp. 363–367). Berkeley, CA: University of California Press.

Sparrow, M. K. (2000). *The regulatory craft: Controlling risks, solving problems and managing compliance*. Washington, DC: Brookings Press.

Stiglitz, J. (2009). Spring is here, but contain your excitement. www.bepress.com/ev

Streeck, W. (1995). Neo-voluntarism: A new European social policy regime? *European Law Journal, 1*, 31–59.

Taylor-Gooby, P. (Ed.). (2004). *New risks, new welfare: The transformation of the European welfare state*. Oxford: Oxford University Press.

Time Magazine, 11 June 2008.

van der Velde, M., & van Houtum, H. (2004). De-politicizing labour market indifference and immobility in the European Union. In O. Kramsch & B. Hooper (Eds.), *Cross-border governance in the European Union*. London: Routledge.

Veggeland, N. (2003). *Det nye demokratiet: et politisk laboratorium for partnerskap [The new democracy: A political laboratory for partnership]*. Kristiansand: Norwegian Academic Press.

Veggeland, N. (2004). *The competitive society: How democratic and effective?* Kristiansand: Norwegian Academic Press.

Veggeland, N. (2005). *Europapolitikk, innenrikspolitikk og kommunene [European politics, domestic politics, and the municipalities]*. Oslo: Kommuneforlaget.

Veggeland, N. (2007). *Paths and public innovation in the global age*. Cheltenham, UK: Edward Elgar.

Veggeland, N. (2009). *Taming the regulatory state: Politics and ethics*. Cheltenham, UK: Edward Elgar.

Vibert, F. (2007). *The rise of the unelected: Democracy and the new separation of powers*. Cambridge: Cambridge University Press.

Wallace, H., Wallace, W., & Pollack, M. A. (2005). *Policy-making in the European Union*. Oxford: Oxford University Press.

Weaver, R. K. (1986). The politics of blame avoidance. *Journal of Public Policy, 6*(4), 371–398.

Chapter 4
The Concept of the Democratic Regulatory State in a Scandinavian Context

Bureaucracy Connotations

The topic of this chapter is the analysis of the concept of the regulatory state in Europe and its impact on Scandinavian democratic welfare state management. The 1970s represents the end of the Keynesian era. When Keynesian economists were looking forward, they saw, based on the experiences of the stagflation crisis in the 1970s, a need for the state to add new instruments for controlling the economy. In their view, there was a need for an incremental expansion of the state's control of the economy. The expected free market expansion would need new regulatory state control to be strengthened through reform. This way of thinking was also endorsed by governments of the Scandinavian countries.

The European context of the regulatory state, as outlined in previous chapters, serves as a term of reference and as a primary context in the analysis of the ideas and concepts of Scandinavian development. Impact analysis normally focuses on the comparison of government structure in Scandinavia with the regulatory EU. In our context, the focus is on national state order transition and impact in the wake of the change from parliamentary government to dominant non-parliamentarian democratic governance of the EU type (Croley 1996). After the Second World War, the social democratic political order dominated the building of the often recommended Scandinavian welfare state. This is sometimes also named the Keynesian Welfare State, because of its economic roots in Keynesianism. John Maynard Keynes (1883–1946) was a British economist whose ideas fundamentally changed the theory and practice of macroeconomics and the economic policies of governments. He built on and greatly refined earlier work on the causes of business cycles and was one of the most influential economists of the twentieth century. Keynes promoted an active interventionist state, which is in contrast to the traditional passive state that accepted free market movements. Both Keynesian economics and social democratic order were challenged in the 1980s by the new wave of neoliberalism, a wave which denied the superiority of the central state and Keynesianism. Expanding global

© Springer Nature Switzerland AG 2020
N. Veggeland, *Democratic Governance in Scandinavia*,
https://doi.org/10.1007/978-3-030-18270-0_4

markets could not remain unregulated: controlling transnational state instruments were needed. The importance of the supranational EU became obvious. Sweden and Finland became full EU member states in 1994, and Norway and Iceland became member states of the European Economic Area (EEA). Denmark had been an EU member since 1972. The regulatory state order arose in Scandinavia.

The traditional social democratic parties in Scandinavia were also very much inspired by the British "New Labour reform" of the 1990s (Veggeland 2018a, b). A regulatory supported free market-based economy and New Public Management (NPM) came to form a major plank of public policy during New Labour's third term in office in the United Kingdom. In 2005, the then Prime Minister Tony Blair argued in a well-publicized speech that there was enormous pressure on decision-makers "to act to eliminate market risk in a way that is out of all proportion to the potential damage" and called for a debate on regulatory means in public policy-making (Blair 2005). Prime Minister Blair, arguing the need to replace the compensation culture of the central state with a common-sense culture of market mechanisms that expose public welfare services to competition with private actors, committed the government to regulatory action to help ensure that creativity and reform in the private and public welfare sectors guaranteed efficiency and productivity. The Scandinavian social democracies, in turn, came up with administrative reforms to replace the ordinary welfare bureaucracy in the wake of such ideological ideas. Bureaucracy refers to both a body of nonelective government officials and an administrative policy-making group, bureaucracy historically being a government administration managed by departments staffed by nonelected officials (Weber 1922). Bureaucracy is the administrative system that governs any large institution, irrespective of whether it is publicly or privately owned. The traditional bureaucratic public administration of the Scandinavian countries, which is organized as centralized hierarchical structures of agencies, came into being and had the authority and responsibility to implement governmental decisions in society. The word bureaucracy has, since its separation from the Weberian bureaucracy context, developed negative connotations. Bureaucracies have been criticized as being inefficient, convoluted, or too inflexible for individuals and for free market transactions. Governments of Scandinavia, which politically accepted this negative approach to ordinary Weberian bureaucracy, initiated replacements—regulatory mechanisms of surveillance and control. The Scandinavian social democratic parties have failed, from the beginning of the 2000s, to implement successful regulatory states and therefore to be in ruling government positions. Even though the existence of the welfare state still costs the taxpayers a huge amount of money, it does prevail. It prospers, but in a transformed form and order. Privatization and market making have become dominant, the different public services gaining a new organizational structure that makes them more like private sector enterprises. These are called arm's-length bodies (OECD 2005a, b), these non-parliamentarian bodies regulating and controlling public and private activities as market actors. A specific problem, however, with this is that social risks such as the development of inequality and regulatory governance are inclined to eliminate transparency, downgrading the importance of social forces and bottom-up initiatives. This is confirmed by the Scandinavian neoliberal reform approach (Veggeland 2017).

It seems to be commonplace today to state that we live in the age of the regulatory state, one which is characterized by privatization of public services, the establishment of quasi-autonomous regulatory authorities, and the formalization of relationships within policy domains (see Loughlin and Mazey 1994; Moran 2002; Veggeland 2010). This questions four broad concerns. Firstly, what are the sources of this supposed rise of the regulatory state in Europe and does it represent a distinct policy development in Scandinavia? Secondly, what has been the "value added" in terms of empirical and analytical insights, in the study of Scandinavian politics (and more broadly European politics)? Thirdly, does the age of the regulatory state constitute a new age of stability of the Scandinavian states? Fourthly, and finally, what is the future of (the study of) the regulatory state?

Regulatory State

A regulatory state that pursues an economic policy that privileges the regulation of market exchanges rejects direct government intervention in terms of Keynesianism (Croley 1996). This challenges the framework of the traditional Scandinavian Keynesian welfare state. The term regulatory state refers to the expansion in the use of law- and rule-making, monitoring and enforcement techniques and institutions by the state, and a parallel change in the way its positive functions in society are performed. The outstanding Italian political economist Giandomenico Majone has made interesting contributions to the understanding of the regulatory state. In 1990, he introduced his research findings in *Deregulation or re-regulation? Regulatory reform in Europe and the United States* (Majone 1990). According to Majone, EU member states delegate certain regulatory powers to the European Commission to insulate themselves from democratic pressures that would inhibit optimal policy outcomes. Regulatory policies are followed up at the European national level, the central state replacing the executive of the Commission. This undermines the control of the elected democratic bodies. We, in this chapter, therefore study regulatory state order in the context of Scandinavian democratic governance.

The expansion of the central state in the 2000s was primarily via regulation implementations and less via taxing and spending (Veggeland 2009). The notion of the regulatory state is becoming increasingly more attractive to theoreticians of the state. This has led to a growth in the use and application of rule-making, monitoring and enforcement strategies, and the parallel growth of market regulation (Majone 1997). The co-expansion of state agencies for welfare, market, and business regulation in the domestic and the European arenas suggests that the notions of regulatory governance and regulatory capitalism are significantly useful in the study of the polities of our time. Important reading on this is the OECD Publishing reports "OECD Principles of Regulatory Quality and Performance" (2005a, b) and "Government Capacity to Assure High Quality Regulation in Sweden" (2007).

The regulatory state concept suggests that the role of the central state, in both the fields of the economy and social issues, is shifting from positive direct intervention to non-parliamentary arm's-length regulation and arbitration, particularly in modern Anglo-Saxon countries. The OECD (2002) names this invention a new form of "distributed public governance." The supposed rise of the regulatory state has thus both a policy and an institutional dimension, the two functioning together. This, in terms of Scandinavian reforms, signals a formal end of Keynesian interventionism as the dominant economic policy paradigm and highlights the creation of new administrative tools to steer the market-exposed public sector and its dynamics.

We see European and Scandinavian governments relying less, from the beginning of the 2000s, on public ownership and direct economic intervention through fiscal and monetary tools for public sector activities, including welfare services (Majone 2006). Reforms increasingly utilize arm's-length regulation to stimulate competition and ensure the provision of welfare goods. The market making of public sector responsibilities was similarly achieved by the government directly running companies in fields such as transportation, telecommunications, post, and welfare. The role of government in these liberalized sectors became one of a neutral controlling instance that ensures competition and social protection, where this is necessary. Welfare offers became something that was made at a distance from users. The transition was not a sweeping deregulation, but rather a complex re-regulation associated with a redefinition of the state's role in the polity (Majone 1990).

The process of delegating regulatory authority to subordinates gained widespread appeal with the New Deal (1933–1939) in the USA (Woolner 2018). This, as already addressed, picked up considerable speed in the 1980s and 1990s. Scandinavian governments also, in forming the regulatory state, developed a set of agencies, commissions, and special courts that develop, monitor, and enforce market rules and that increasingly shape policy at home and abroad (OECD 2007). Regulatory agencies could set policy claims, specify regulatory frameworks, and punish noncompliance. The powers and resources delegated and made available to these arm's-length institutions furthermore affected the state's capacity to shape policy implementation. The amount of public capital involved in implementation made it attractive to private actors to carry out the assignments, financed by public authorities. This meant privatization and the replacement of public actors, a growing trend that we observe in Scandinavia, for example in health and elderly care. Furthermore, the public and private arm's-length bodies increasingly took advantage of their domestic autonomy to work with external third parties, spearheading a new form of networking governance rooted in global networks.

Analysis of contemporary welfare states has focused on the intervention of the public regulatory administration to provide protection and security to citizens. It follows that the areas exposed to regulation are manifold. A list is provided below of the areas to help readers gain an overview of this diversity. All can be found in the Scandinavian countries.

Areas of Regulatory Exposure

- Advertising regulation
- Alcoholic beverages
- Bank regulation
- Consumer protection
- Cyber-security regulation
- Economic regulation
- Financial regulation
- Food safety and food security
- International agreements
- Noise regulation
- Nuclear safety
- Minerals
- Occupational safety and health
- Public health
- Labor marked regulation
- Regulation and monitoring of pollution
- Regulation of acupuncture
- Regulation of nanotechnology
- Regulation of sport
- Regulation of therapeutic goods
- Regulation through litigation
- Regulation on pollution
- Regulation and prevalence of homeopathy
- Regulation of science
- Transportation regulation
- Vehicle regulation
- Wage regulation
- Welfare regulation
- Weapon regulation

Some literature describes the regulatory state order as a fast and flexible alternative to the cumbersome and overly bureaucratic strategies of the previous polity (Keen 2017). Its emergence raises a number of important questions about democratic governance, accountability and the role of public powers, and the loss of this. Keynesian policies were generally proposed and adopted by elected executives and legislatures. We now, however, increasingly see the development of laws, regulations, and partnership agreements outside parliamentary processes, implemented by unelected technocratic arm's-length bodies, which in the framework of the OECD (2005a, b) are described as "distributed public governance."

The outcome of this is a growing democratic deficit. To advocates, this mode of governance took the politics out of market regulation, this, to skeptics, being precisely the problem (Piketty 2014). David Bach and Abraham Newman (2018) are clear that whereas the independence granted to new regulatory institutions was supposed to buffer them from capture by political and business interests, it also threatened to isolate them from direct democratic control. This dynamic was most pronounced at the international level, where projects suffered from a legitimacy deficit that many analysts attributed to the democratic deficit of arm's-length regulatory institutions.

Consequences of Regulatory Governance

Arm's-length regulatory agencies in Scandinavia are typically executive bodies that belong indirectly to the government and that have the statutory authority to perform their functions under the oversight of the legislative authorities. Their actions are generally open to legal review. Scandinavian academics talk of "law-making of politics" (Veggeland 2017).

As the list above shows, regulatory agencies deal in manifold areas of adminis trative law, regulatory law, secondary legislation, and rule-making. The existence of independent regulatory agencies is justified by the complexity of certain regulatory and supervisory tasks and the drawbacks of political interference. In Scandinavia, as in the EU, some independent regulatory agencies implement adopted administrative reform and carry out audits. For example, a company or organization must obtain a license to operate from a regulator before it can enter an industry. This license will set out the conditions which the companies or organizations operating within the industry must adhere to. Regulatory bodies also, in some instances, have powers to require that companies or organizations operating within a particular industry adjust to certain standards. This type of regulation is common in the provision of public and private welfare services, which are subject to standard regulation. It challenges the soft characteristics of the traditional Scandinavian welfare state's way of offering people a helping hand.

The rise of autonomous regulatory power has had profound consequences. It has enabled governments to diversify executive democracy and to partake directly in the everyday affairs of millions of citizens and businesses. The European Union helps the Scandinavian countries to produce thousands of regulations every year (see Appendix B). This is not much compared with the U.S. *Code of Federal Regulations*, which runs to 165,000 pages and contains tens of thousands of rules involving every conceivable aspect of commerce and society. In the EU, the costs of implementing regulations are covered by each single member state. Many regulations are relatively minor and uncontroversial. Some, however, fall into the "major rule" category with great costs. The exercise of regulatory power has yielded important benefits. It has contributed significantly to the reduction in air pollution and health and aesthetic improvements, safeguarded welfare services, and protected labor market conditions. But regulation, like all forms of concentrated power, is exposed to excess and abuse, also in Scandinavia. A general problem is that the health, safety, and environmental agencies regularly set standards which involve costs that exceed any plausible measure of their benefits. A specific problem of regulation is that regulatory governance is inclined to eliminate transparency and downgrades the importance of social forces and bottom-up initiatives, as has been confirmed by studies.

Regulatory legislation is public and symbolic. In Scandinavia, democratic governance is characterized by hearings, speeches, and votes where the people's representatives declare themselves for or against policy matters. This could, for example, be social policies, environmental policies, or discrimination against the handicapped. Regulatory administration, in contrast, is cloistered and distant, characterized by piecework rule-making, interest groups maneuvering, and impenetrable complexity. No single authority is able to claim to have full insight into the piecework of regulations and the effects of their functioning together (Veggeland 2010). Even when initial legislation faces strong opposition, the opponents quickly master the program's administration and accommodate themselves to its requirements. Arm's-length's agencies try to maintain coalitions of program "stakeholders" that often resist outside threats of reform. Outside threats are, furthermore, likely to be feeble. Regulatory policies are largely insensible to the general public involvement and mostly impact the operation of public services, business firms, and other intermediate organizations.

Instances of excess and abuse are cause enough for alarm. Regulation is, however, also problematic within its prescribed democratic bounds, particularly with respect to the traditional democratic order, including in Scandinavia. We can examine reforms that have brought regulatory authorities into powerful positions, positions that have evolved from our reference to the OECD's (2002) concept of "distributed public governance." The autonomous authorities in Scandinavia do not directly execute "democratic government by the people." Their output perspective, in contrast, tends to emphasize "government for the people" (Scharpf 1999: 6). Not representative in the classical democratic sense, autonomous regulatory authorities dominate political arenas such as in the European Union and member states in Europe. Their legitimacy depends on output achievements and represents a form of steering by objectives (Lane 2000). Contextually, Fritz Scharpf adds that (1999: 27): "It may be an exaggeration to conclude that this implies "the end of democracy," but the loss of authentic and effective self-determination seems significant and visible enough to explain the present sense of malaise in democratic politics." Reforms since the 1980s have created the regulatory state and its institutions. Reliance on regulation rather than parliamentary decision-making, public ownership, centralized planning, or administration characterizes the methods of the regulatory state (Majone 1997; Veggeland 2010). It is decisive, however, that the execution of governance by the institutions of the regulatory state in some way is rooted in the will of the people. In Scandinavia and Europe, we see a new form of governance that embraces the democratic deficit. Maybe it is this approach the great American political scientist Robert Dahl is thinking of, when writing (1989: 350): "[N]ew democracy in a world we can already dimly foresee are certain to be radically unlike the limits and possibilities of democracy in any previous time or space." We may suggest the following configuration of different concepts appearing across the modern polity.

The Scandinavian parliamentary government with the governance systems of the new democracy expresses a great step toward an unknown ruling future (Veggeland 2015). The classic democracy of origin does not, following Robert Dahl's suggestion, exist anymore in the modern Western world. The rise of the regulatory state has generated a mixed-up model. In some national states, such as the Scandinavian countries, there is an administrative tradition of the subordination of regulatory institutions to governmental authorities. In other countries, such as the Anglo-Saxon countries and the EU, there is an administrative tradition of giving preference to regulatory state institutions as arm's-length bodies (Knill 2001; Veggeland 2007). This is fundamentally about whether preference is given to democratic government by the people or to regulatory-based governance. For example, the European community in its very beginning, i.e., from 1952/1957 until its first direct election of representatives to the Parliament in 1979, became essentially based on an autocratic system. The nonelected representatives of the Council of Ministers decided regulations, regulations being implemented by the regulatory institution of the Commission of the Community (Kjær 2004; Veggeland 2010). After the Maastricht Treaty of 1992, the EU was transformed by reforms and characterized by a distributed governance system consisting of both supreme nonelected agencies and supreme elected representatives in the Parliament. A new democracy was, therefore, introduced (Veggeland 2003).

Our regulatory state is the product of more than a century of institutional evolution in the Western world. It is also resilient and adaptable to the EU-friendly Scandinavian countries, and will not easily be tamed (Veggeland 2010; Dahl 1989). The essence of the rise of the regulatory state replacing parliamentary governance is, as we have seen, however autonomous executive power, distributed governance. This tells us where we must start, with the checking and balancing powers of democratic "governance by the people" and arm's-length "governance for the people" (Scharpf 1999). European integration shoulders much of the blame for fostering regulatory power in the first place in Scandinavia and is seldom nimble enough to check member state's cases of excess. In recent years, legislators have tried repeatedly to countermand controversial rule-making initiatives, such as free migration, social policies, and threats to welfare state sustainability.

Social Capital of the Scandinavian Type

The OECD (2005a, b) once ranked the Scandinavia welfare state at the top of the list of "social capital" as the basic condition for good governance. The outcomes are numerically marked as economic stability, low unemployment, social security, and high standard of living. In this sense, the Scandinavian countries are in focus as heavy social capital holders carrying good governance. What is "social capital"? "It is the ability of people to work together for common purposes in groups and organizations" according to the American economist Francis Fukuyama (1995). "Social capital can be further defined simply as the existence of a certain set of informal values or norms shared among members of a group that permit cooperation among them" (Fukuyama 1999).

Robert Putnam agrees with the concept that trust, norms, and networks can improve the efficiency of society by facilitating coordinated actions (Putnam 1993). He furthermore widens the concept, emphasizing the importance of people's involvement within informal activities and voluntarily participating or being part of voluntary associations. However, despite the importance of social capital, Putnam has claimed there is a decrease in public participation in these informal activities and voluntary associations in societies such as the Scandinavian, this having a negative impact on social cohesion. He writes that we have, over the past 30 years, become ever more alienated from one another and from our social and political institutions and that this disengagement poses a critical threat to our personal health, local communities, and national well-being (Putnam 1993). He believes it will take 30 years for regulatory state order to rise in the Anglo-American world, including Scandinavia. This order has rubbed the social democratic founded universal welfare state which just generated the attractive social capital.

In this perspective, we can view the social capital of the Scandinavian countries of today as a transformation of the traditional welfare state capacity established in the years after the Second World War to that now named regulatory social capital out from the transformed Scandinavian regulatory model (Veggeland 2007). We are here talking of a specific concept: "Scandinavian flexicurity policy." Flexicurity is an integrated strategy for simultaneously enhancing *flexibility and security* in the labor market. It attempts to reconcile employers' need for a flexible workforce with workers' need for security, their confidence in that they will not face long periods of unemployment. Flexicurity is a welfare state model with a proactive labor market policy. The term was first used by the social democratic former Prime Minister of Denmark Poul Nyrup Rasmussen in the 1990s. The term refers to the combination of a regulated labor market flexibility in a dynamic economy with security and universal welfare for all, including workers. The Government of Denmark explicitly expressed flexicurity as entailing a "golden triangle" with a "three-sided mix of flexibility in the labor market combined with social security and active labor market politics."

Presented contextually, Scandinavian social flexicurity claims collective action and long-term embracing policies of both economic and social characters. The driving force is a path-dependent political will to sustain a national partnership between the regulatory authorities, the unions of employees and of employers, and the people. The goal is good governance in the forms of universal social security, institutional stability, and economic and competitive advantages. Universal social security lays the foundation for the development of flexible labor markets that all partners benefit from in different ways, including benefits irreducible to economic factors.

The Scandinavia Active Labor Market Policy (ALMP) is another expensive public contribution to the social capital of the grand partnership and the flexicurity concept. ALMP is an important part of the state authorities' responsibility for planning, building, restoring, and protecting human capital and for making human resources the basic element of partnerships and social-capital building. ALMPs compel, through regulatory innovations, a range of public means and measures to function together. The execution of these means and measures must, furthermore, take place within the framework of the universal welfare state model. The mechanisms behind the regulatory Scandinavian flexicurity are as follows (Nilsson 2018).

- Universal welfare and social security allows employees to feel free to move and change jobs and partners, safety and equal access to welfare rule being independent of geography, position, employer, and network attachment.
- ALMP performs collaborative governance by complex partnership policies (social capital) and by education, individual training, and lifelong learning (human capital). The performance not only involves the public sector, but also partners across all sectors, from public services to private actors to NGOs.
- Scandinavian flexicurity is a nationally implemented policy concept, but is also fundamental to partnership-building and regional development capacities domestically and across borders. Flexicurity reproduces long-term partnership arrangements, an effective labor market, high labor productivity, high employment rates, and a high level of social and human capital.

Scandinavian flexicurity is, as an important part of the social capital concept, expensive and imposes a high tax burden on the citizens. Even so, the policy sustains its legitimacy from its double efficiency of returning economic revenues and social security. Comparative figures suggestive of the OECD data were made available in the 2004 World Economic Forum report on the Lisbon Agenda (WEF). In a European perspective, these figures revealingly showed that if the Anglo-Saxon USA was, for comparative purposes, an EU member state, it would rank fourth behind three existing member states on an overall assessment of economic competitiveness. Remarkably, the top countries, Denmark, Sweden, Finland, Norway, and Iceland, were all Nordic/Scandinavian states.

The consistent performance of the Scandinavian social capital is striking across a range of indicators (Veggeland 2016).

- Economic growth
- Labor productivity
- Active Labor Market Policy (ALMP)
- Labor-market flexibility but social security, called "flexicurity"
- Regional and local development policy
- Research and development investment
- Performance in the high-tech and telecom sectors
- Rates of employment (including among women and older workers)

In this context, social capital as flexicurity turns out to be not only "capital" but also "welfare." Jan-Evert Nilsson is indeed right in his statements to take Sweden as the point of departure. Countries in the Scandinavian region provide greater welfare and social capital to its citizens than other countries.

Looked upon basically, social capital building may promote good governance and long-term positive consequences in one polity context, but in another context it may turn out very differently. From the analysis of this chapter, we learn that flexicurity does influence the quality and practical outcome of the regulatory state. The Scandinavian model and its social capital are, however, drifting. The maintenance of path-dependent collective responsibility is threatened (Timonen 2004). Thus, as "social capital" has become an economic capital term in the era of the regulatory state, it seems that flexicurity likewise is threatened by the same shift of connotation away from a policy for national universal welfare. In the political debate (even in the Scandinavian countries), the economic connotation is given superiority as a policy for increasing European and national market competitiveness and economic growth rather than for keeping the policy as a steady path to good welfare policy in the global age. The flexicurity policy faces serious challenges today from the embracing of labor migration for an integrated borderless Europe. The focus tends to change from the social connotation to an economic connotation, followed by regulatory challenges (Streeck 1995).

Controversial Scandinavia

What accounts for the Scandinavian countries' path-dependent, strong democratic, and soft regulated universal welfare state, which today is in transition to a hard regulatory order?

There is a reason why the Scandinavian welfare states are still the envy of many across the world (Veggeland 2017). Even decades into a state regulatory project to reform them, Scandinavian politics still achieves relatively high-income equality, large tax-financed welfare programs, powerful collective unions, and relatively low unemployment rates.

Neoliberal politicians tell us that the only way to societal prosperity is through low tax rates, deregulated business, and cutthroat competitive labor markets. Yet, despite failing to meet the metrics of the Anglo-American variety of regulatory capitalism, Scandinavian countries stubbornly continue to prosper and regularly come out on top of the global indexes of happiness and quality of life (World Happiness Report 2018).

It is no surprise, therefore, to find neoliberals and conservatives devoting considerable intellectual energy to delegitimizing the original "Scandinavian model" of public welfare.

In 2018, the Institute of Economic Affairs, a British neoliberal think tank, devoted an entire book to Scandinavian "un-exceptionalism." (IEA 2018). The aim was to downward estimate the success story of the Scandinavian welfare states, arguing in classical neoliberal terms of a fashion of the success of the Scandinavian countries in the policy era of public welfare, and that anything exceptional and successful about it had vanished since then. This is because all Western countries, including the Scandinavian, were involved in the wave of growing international regulatory state formations. The wave makes national states converge, similarity in administrative structure being the outcome. From this fact follows that the Scandinavian welfare state has been reformed and is no longer controversial in an international framework.

Meanwhile in the USA, where the campaign of the socialist Bernie Sanders has thrown ideas of Scandinavian social democracy into the political mainstream, the National Review's Kevin Williamson has adopted the opposite strategy when writing "We Can't Afford It" (2019). Here he acknowledges the continuing exceptionalism of the Nordic experience and admits that the Nordic countries have indeed been relatively successful until the very recent rise of the regulatory state following neoliberal ideas of the market making of public welfare services.

The modernized Scandinavian welfare state of today is controversial in a political sense, as the regulatory concept is controversial in the European integration in general. Other chapters in this book reveal a long range of interest conflicts in the wake of the regulatory state administrative way of ruling, distributing governance, and sharing social goods. The universal welfare state of Scandinavia has, however, great support from citizens, from the people (Nilsson 2017). The Scandinavian welfare state exists somewhere between democratic governance "by the people" and new democratic governance "for the people," with reference to Scharpf (1999). It gains legitimacy from both parliamentary inputs and outputs. Today, the universal welfare state sustains egalitarian labor markets and is so popular among voters that even liberal or conservative politicians who want to dismantle them have to run as defenders of public welfare if they wish to avoid electoral suicide. This situation did not emerge from the mists of history. It is the product of decades of struggle by organized labor and other popular movements throughout the twentieth century.

The social-democratic welfare state has faced strong historical challenges, both from the Left, by strong communist and new left movements, and from the Right, by organized business, such as the powerful employer organizations in all the five countries.

Progressives might say they want to adopt Scandinavian-style institutional models of public universal welfare. But Williamson (2019) informs us, with a hefty dose of hermeneutics of suspicion, that citizens don't like ethnic diversity. Maybe this is true. But it is a superficial accusation. In any case, the premise of Williamson's masked attempt to racialize the Scandinavian success story is flawed. Williamson also writes that the nations of Northern Europe were, until recently, ethnically homogeneous, overwhelmingly white, hostile to immigration, nationalistic, and frankly racist in much of their domestic policy.

Scandinavia is not exceptional by European standards when it comes to racism and nationalism, and one can readily find examples of hostility to immigration, chauvinistic nationalism, and racist policies in the histories of the Scandinavian countries. For example, and like most European countries, anti-semitism was bad in Scandinavian countries before World War II, and nationalist mindfulness swept through all of the Scandinavian countries in the nineteenth century, as it did around the world (see new Norwegian study on prewar anti-semitism (Michelet 2018).

Williamson fails to firstly prove that the Nordic countries, irrespective of whether we are talking about state policy or popular sentiment, really do have a consistently worse record than other countries, and secondly that racism played any part in the establishment of the Scandinavian-style universal welfare states in the twentieth century. However, today authorities avoid the term "immigrant," using instead "persons of migrant origin" in official discourse. A policy of diversity management was introduced some years ago to counteract tendencies of social exclusion and stereotyping. More strength has been put into the previously rather weak laws on ethnic specific rights, such as the need to learn Scandinavian languages.

In sum, Williamson's case presenting the Nordic model as inherently racist is weak at best. It is certainly true that the Nordic countries today all have sizable right-wing populist movements dominated by xenophobic sentiment. But this is equally true for most other European countries.

The Regulatory Clientelism Turn

Social democracy, as a ruling ideology in Scandinavia, has become weak under the era of regulatory state order despite its socioeconomic approach advocating the welfare state concept and the demand for social and geographical distribution and redistribution toward a more just and solidary society. It loses because it does not confront capitalism's history and structural features rooted in market mechanisms and our social capital concept. It is interesting to study the work of Francis Fuku-yama, such as *Political Order and Political Decay: From the Industrial Revolution to the Present Day* (2007) and also *Identity: The Demand for Dignity and the Politics of Resentment* (2018). We see a strong tendency of politicians and ideologies to wipe out their own path of common sense and traditions and instead submit to positive regulations. Only the empirically judicial given is, however, true and right. Enduring social structures are welcome, only because they outline statistically. All empirical evidence shows that capital and its wealth accumulation end up in the hands of a handful of rich players in the social and geographical centre, at the expense of the many in the periphery. We observe the following also occurring in Scandinavia. The periphery's population is transforming into clients living on allowance as a result of a lack of business infrastructure or a personal disability diagnosis. We see, from official statistics, that one percent of the population has become owners of most of the country's wealth and value creation, a fact shown over again regularly. We know this as empirical evidence. But this does not have to be the case with regard to a worthwhile, good society of welfare offers. Let us examine some historical ideological roots of value for the understanding of Scandinavian social clientelism.

First, we can talk about what is commonly referred to as "cultural puritanism," which is linked to the building of capital, including social capital, in the hands of the economic elites. We must go back to the years of 1500–1600 Europe and the emergence of religious extremism that stemmed from the teachings of Luther and Calvin. Their thinking was rooted in the belief in predestination: that everything was planned in advance by God in terms of who would end in heaven and who would end in hell. It was quite simple. As a reflection of this, it was the will of God that determined who became rich and who became poor and who became successful and who failed. Success was a divine omen and testimony, for which there was empirical evidence. Through the centralization and accumulation of capital and wealth, God's determination could be demonstrated for all to watch. It created demonstrable industrialization, growth, and justice through law-making from supreme authorities. The puritan supernatural belief justified the enormous differences between rich and poor, between the center and the periphery, and between rich countries and poor developing countries. It was also consistent with "Protestant Work Ethics." The poor were simply demonstrably lazy and the only ones able of initiating aimless revolts, the belief being that they made no contribution to the social capital of the time. In order to prevent potential rebellion and the emergence of revolutionary social movements, the rich followed the path of clientelism by providing demonstrable and calculated money assistance to the poor and to the periphery in return for loyalty. The poor relief funds emerged and executive authority was given to municipalities, causing rising governmental budgets. Furthermore, the welfare state placated the working class and the poor into becoming voters as social democrats. Out of this came the social clientelism and the growth of social democratic parties.

However, it is here in this modern Scandinavian regulatory welfare state that social democracy meets its opposition and weakening effects (Streeck 1995). Industry workers, farmers, and civil servants in Scandinavia and Europe are no longer satisfied with their statistical status as regulated social-democratic clients. They refocus on social inequality, on a hard-pressed, goal-oriented working life, on the weakening of the unions, and the centralization of power and institutions, and a weakened representative democracy (Nilsson 2017, 2018). Under the constraint of positive regulatory denial of predictable future hope, they become politically passive and disappear into right-wing populist movements and political parties. In this world, migration is blamed for creating empirically demonstrable inequality and not as an effect of regulatory capitalism.

This turn is not random, according to Fukuyama. It seems to be built upon historical Social Darwinism. Immigrant groups and migrants are very poor compared to national welfare clients, and according to Social Darwinism, the poor are poor for genetic reasons, caused by evolution-based competition and the "survival of the fittest." According to the right-wing populists, the foreign migrant groups are therefore given no hope of future integration and of becoming new useful future labor. They will remain costly clients, moochers. People of color in the United States are pointed to as empirical evidence, their background as slaves and their power being defined as genetically inferior, many remaining a largely disintegrated and discriminated subclass.

But how can Social Darwinism survive in our enlightened society? We cannot go into detailed and profound answers, but rather point out the fact that in our time, justice evidence generated by the regulatory state is used as the basis for all the surveillance and control of psyche and society. The regulatory state approach is widely accepted and is in itself an ideology. It always supports the enduring situation and confirms judicial rights. It also always supports the idea of technology's blessing, the benefits of centralization for economic growth, and the ever-existing clients, which in turn depend on capital's liquidity and the market's expansion nationally and internationally. This theory also positively confirms that the competitive advantage of regulatory innovations is created on the basis of human and social capital and competing social elite hierarchies. Based on statistics, the notion emerges that skill and winning instincts are genetic, but also determined by varying social environments, and that only some individuals and groups of people have the right social and personal qualities.

This has become a convincing fact-based belief. It is established as empirically true, in this competition between social groups and states, that losers are to a large extent created, an expanding periphery leading to the loss of development potential and social capital. The rich and skilled in the center are the winners and must be politically rewarded, for example, by tax reductions so they can become even richer and more successful. Client status is confirmed: social and welfare support schemes and subsidies that save the reformed welfare state are also statistically demonstrated. In the meantime, social democracy loses political power. It is empirically established, without any actual path out of the conundrum being offered. Lastly, regulatory governance belief only rejects predictions that cannot be statistically demonstrated or confirmed.

The famous French economist, Professor Thomas Piketty, with his 2013 bestseller *Capital in the Twenty-First Century*, is again of relevance with a new research report on social inequality. In this, he describes how inequality increases in Europe and the EU and demonstrates, using statistics, how social capital declines and clientelism spreads in the EU and in Scandinavia. People are affected and life sustainability is deconstructed. This also affects political choices. It is no longer the situation that people with low education and low income, primarily social security beneficiaries and clients, vote for left-wing parties. Instead, a large proportion of left-wing voters are characterized as people with high education and high incomes. At the same time, an economic upper class with large fortunes vote for right-wing parties, as has always been the case. Piketty describes the new reality as follows: "We have gradually moved from a class-based party system to something I suggest calling a multi-elite system". Thus, the battle between parties of the political right and left, also in Scandinavia, is basically a battle between two elites: one with higher education and high income and another with both high income and wealth. Both of these ruling groups stand for a policy based on the regulatory defense of existing power in terms of OECD's distributed public governance and hard regulated social clientelism.

References

Bach, D., & Newman, A. (2018). *European regulatory power: Capacity and sequencing in international pharmaceutical and cosmetics governance*, aln24@georgetown.edu

Blair, T. (2005). *Tony Blair's conference speech 2005*. London: UK News.

Croley, S. P. (1996). The administrative procedure act and regulatory reform: A reconciliation. *Administrative Law Journal, 10*(1), 35–49.

Dahl, R. A. (1989). *Who governs? Democracy and power in an American city*. New Haven, CT: Yale University Press.

Fukuyama, F. (1995). *Trust: The social virtues and the creation of prosperity*. New York: Free Press.

Fukuyama, F. (1999). *The great disruption: Human nature and the reconstitution of social order*. New York: Free Press.

Fukuyama, F. (2007). *Political order and political decay: From the industrial revolution to the present day*. New York: Free Press.

Fukuyama, F. (2018). *Identity: The demand for dignity and the politics of resentment*. New York: Free Press.

IEA. (2018). *Institute of Economic Affairs Analysis Report*, London.

Keen, S. (2017). *Can we avoid another financial crisis?* Amazon.com.

Kjær, A. M. (2004). *Governance*. Cambridge: Cambridge University Press.

Knill, C. (2001). *The Europeanization of the national administrations*. Cambridge: Cambridge University Press.

Lane, J.-E. (2000). *New public management*. London: Routledge.

Loughlin, J., & Mazey, S. (1994). *The end of the French unitary state? Ten years of regionalization I France*. London: Frank Cass.

Majone, G. (1990). *Deregulation or re-regulation? Regulatory reform in Europe and the United States*. New York: St. Martin's Press.

Majone, G. (1997). From the positive to the regulatory state. Causes and consequences of change in the mode of government. *Journal of Public Policy, 17*(3), 139–189.

Majone, G. (2006). *Regulating Europe. Routledge research in European public policy*. London: Taylor & Francis.

Michelet, M. (2018). *Hva visste hjemmefronten?* Oslo: Gyldendal.

Moran, M. (2002). *The British regulatory state: High modernism and hyper-innovation*. Oxford: Oxford University Press.

Nilsson, J. E. (2017). The social democratic welfare model: A child of times past. In N. Veggeland (Ed.), *Administrative strategies of our time*. New York: Nova Science.

Nilsson, J. E. (2018). New Keynesian policy: The revival of each policy maker's dream. In N. Veggeland (Ed.), *Keynesian policies—A new deal in the European narrative. Employment, equality and sustainability*. New York: Nova Science.

OECD. (2002). *Distributed public governance: Agencies, authorities and other government bodies*. Paris: OECD.

OECD. (2005a). *Modernizing government. The way forward*. Paris: OECD.

OECD. (2005b). *Guiding principles for regulatory quality and performance*. Paris: OECD.

OECD. (2007). *Government capacity to assure high quality regulation in Sweden*. Paris: OECD.

Piketty, T. (2014). *Capital in the twenty-first century*. Cambridge, MA: Harvard University Press.

Putnam, R. D. (1993). *Making democracy work*. Princeton, NJ: Princeton University Press.

Scharpf, F. (1999). *Governing in Europe: Effective and democratic*. Oxford: Oxford University Press.

Streeck, W. (1995). Neo-voluntarism: A new European social policy regime? *European Law Journal, 1*, 31–59.

Timonen, S. (2004). New risks—Are they still new for the Nordic welfare states? In P. Taylor-Gooby (Ed.), *New risks, new welfare: The transformation of the European welfare state* (pp. 83–110). Oxford: Oxford University Press.

Veggeland, N. (2003). *Det Nye Demokratiet. Et politisk laboratorium for partnerskap*. Kristiansand: Høyskoleforlaget.

Veggeland, N. (2007). *Paths of public innovation in the global age: Lessons from Scandinavia*. Cheltenham, UK: Edward Elgar.

Veggeland, N. (2009). *Taming the regulatory state: Politics and ethics*. Cheltenham, UK: Edward Elgar.

Veggeland, N. (2010). *Den nye reguleringsstaten. Idébrytninger og styringskonflikter.* Oslo: Gyldendal Akademisk.

Veggeland, N. (2015). *Regulatory governance.* Published online as text book/academic book, Bookboon.com, Copenhagen.

Veggeland, N. (Ed.). (2016). *The current Nordic welfare state model.* New York: Nova Science.

Veggeland, N. (Ed.). (2017). *Administrative strategies of our time.* New York: Nova Science.

Veggeland, N. (2018a). Economic crises: A Keynesian new deal perspective. In N. Veggeland (Ed.), *Keynesian policies—A new deal in the European narrative. Employment, equality and sustainability.* New York: Nova Science.

Veggeland, N. (2018b). *Keynesian policies—A new deal in the European narrative. Employment, equality and sustainability.* New York: Nova Science.

Weber, M. (1922). *Wirtschaft und Gesellschaft. Grundriß der verstehenden Soziologie.* Berkeley, CA: University of California Press. Translated to English.

Williamson, K. (2019). *We can't afford it.* Posted in Opinion, US Opinion.

Woolner, D. B. (2018). Franklin D. Roosevelt: The reluctant Keynesian. In N. Veggeland (Ed.), *Administrative strategies of our time.* New York: Nova Science.

World Happiness Report. (2018). *World happiness report.* An annual publication of the United Nations. New York: UN.

Chapter 5
Democracy: A Changing Term

> *Whatever form it takes, the democracy of our successors will not and cannot be the democracy of our predecessors. Nor should it be. For the limits and possibilities of democracy in a world we can already foresee are certain to be radically unlike the limits and possibilities of democracy in any previous time or space* (Dahl 1989: 340)

The Scandinavian democratic governance structure as described above mirrors this famous cited reflection of Robert A. Dahl. It has global value. Robert A. Dahl, who wrote the classic political science work *Who Governs? Democracy and Power in an American City* (1989), presented in his analysis a traditional perception of democracy as a "government by the people." However, based on his empirical analysis of political power in USA's New Haven, Connecticut, he learned that power is, in a democracy, far from unambiguously linked to political elections. The presumption in elections is one citizen, one voice, and with this the equal distribution of power between citizens. Numerical democracy has its limitations. He coined the concept of "political resources" as a background to his empirical conclusions and demonstrated that these resources are unevenly distributed between citizens, cities, and society in general. Social class, knowledge, money, speech, and writing skills represent such unequally distributed political resources.

Dahl built his theory of political resources on empirical data of who succeeded in getting their cases adopted and implemented by majority voting, i.e., in a positive decision-making process. This is, of course, an important aspect of democratic governance. However, it was soon pointed out that another aspect could be equally important, namely, preventing cases from making it up onto the agenda, a kind of negative decision-making process (Bachrach and Baratz 1972). Political strategies are chosen with the goal of blocking them from being actualized. Alternatively, issues and topics are deliberately concealed so that the question of decision-making never comes up in a positive sense. They are "talked away" and denied as reality. The reasons can be varied. For example, strong interests may be at stake, fearing a negative outcome if debate and voting were to take place. Political resources are used

N. Veggeland, *Democratic Governance in Scandinavia*,
https://doi.org/10.1007/978-3-030-18270-0_5

in a negative context, plenty of examples of this being also found in the context of social planning (Innes and Booher 2010).

In a later work (1989) "Democracy and its Critics," Dahl points out another relationship that goes far beyond the question of positive and negative decision-making processes. He claims that modern society's development, nationally and globally, has changed the very foundations of traditional national democracy. It has been completely transformed and will not be able to regain its original form. Transformation will continue and new formulas will be formed that will constitute the starting point for many different models. He also refers to historical development processes, these indicating that this was similar in earlier times. The classical democracy developed in ancient Greece had its territorial and demographic background. Entities were territorially very small, were independent states, and had a culturally unified population (people = demos = ethnos[1]). Direct democracy could therefore be practiced[2] with open squares as arenas where people met, discussed, and made decisions. The regulatory state does not deny this opportunity or undermine its importance as an arena for fair decision-making. Only top-down regulatory governance is acceptable.

The bottom-up formula could no longer be followed politically after the emergence of the nation state and with the introduction of Westphalian sovereignty in Europe after the signature of the peace treaties in 1648. Political units had become territorially and demographically too large and complex. A strong national central power had been the first to be established, and the period of enlightened absolutism began. Later, after the French Revolution in 1789, the formula was transformed into what we know as the indirect representative democracy, based on elections where people exercised their influence through voting. The people (demos) chose their representatives to their national assemblies and were protected against the abuse of power by a national constitution. This is called nation building, and is a development toward what is commonly referred to as "mass democracy" (universal suffrage), based on democratic governance and power sharing: a legislature, the parliament, an executive power authority, the government, and a judiciary—the courts. In Scandinavian Norway, after independence from Denmark, this government formula was initiated in 1814 with Norway's own constitution and a representative parliament, a government, and a Supreme Court (Fig. 5.1).

The "parliamentary chain of government" (Olsen 1978, 1980) can be illustrated as in Fig. 5.1: a sovereign people elects its representatives and decides its laws. These are implemented by the executive authority, the government and its administrative apparatus, and a judiciary (the courts of law) which interprets laws and monitors compliance. In unitary states such as Norway or Denmark, the Supreme Court is the judiciary. In federal states such as Germany or the US, the Supreme Court is entrusted with this task. The Supreme Court is responsible for preventing

---

[1]Demos is the Greek term of "a people." Ethnos is the Greek term for a culturally unified people.

[2]The social order at the time was one in which only free Greek men were represented, not women or slaves.

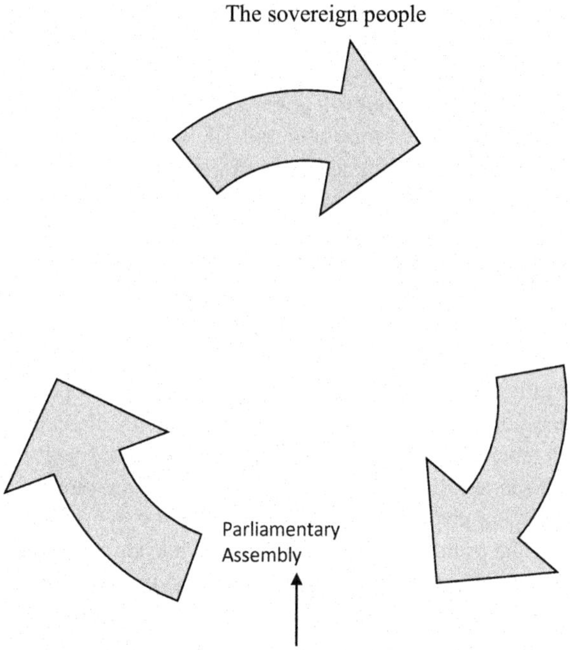

Fig. 5.1 The parliamentary
chain of governance

The sovereign people

Parliamentary
Assembly

the legislative authorities from making decisions that violate the constitution. The constitution limits this authority.

Majority decisions that violate the constitution are invalid. This power is exerted in democratic states in, for example, matters of liberal rights such as freedom of speech and freedom of belief, or oppression of minorities, or discrimination based on gender or sexual orientation. Both democratic legitimacy and fundamental legality are thus secured.

In spite of the metamorphosis of the classic formula for direct democracy, the new indirect form was also perceived, and termed, as democracy, although ancient Greeks might have characterized this indirect form as undemocratic. Both forms are, after all, forms of democracy in that their legitimacy and legality stemmed from governance by the people and the judiciary.

This process has continued up to the present day and a new metamorphosis has been triggered, one that can be termed *post-national democracy* in the wake of the rise of the regulatory state. Internationalization and European integration have provided the basis for further transformation of the democratic formula. Robert A. Dahl does not go further in his analysis in his study, but offers that new formulas for democracy will inevitably be introduced into an increasingly globalized world.

The post-national democracy, based on the principles of the regulatory state which exercises power on the basis of legislation and international and national agreements, has changed traditional democracy and its formula. One example is Norway. Here, the EU has de facto become the fourth level of authority through the European Economic Area Agreement (EEA) and the EU's legislation, regulations, and decisions regarding these being made independent of the Norwegian Parliament. The Keynesian planning state has also been hollowed out by processes of organizational devolution and replaced by the establishment of New Public Management (NPM) at all levels of government. We are also familiar with the processes of contemporary Europe and the EU's regulatory political order. The formula for representative indirect democracy has been transformed into post-national democracy, also called "the new democracy" (Veggeland 2003).

The new democracy in Europe is characterized by governance and power being rooted in three (in federal states 4) territorial units of different sizes: municipality, regional, and state levels (plus the federal level). The territorial state, the nation, continues to largely base its democracy and its democratic legitimacy on laws and decisions taken in indirectly elected assemblies. But internationalization and integration have also created a large territorial European political entity, the EU, which includes 27 nation states plus 3 states with EEA membership. Here, representative democracy cannot function in the traditional sense. The representative European Parliament has strengthened its political position in the European integration, yet does not provide EU legitimacy based on democratic governance.

The principle of subsidiarity was introduced into the EU by the 1994 Maastricht Treaty. The term is historically derived from the universal and "boundless" Catholic Church's governance and the exercise of its religious power. The term is also not foreign to the Roman Empire's method of governing its provinces and vassals. Direct democratic governance in the empire, a formula that they could historically and theoretically have taken from ancient Greece, was virtually impossible. The political units that the Roman Empire took over became territorially too large and populated, too diverse and culturally complex, for the practice of democratically based governance. The Romans were familiar with the Greek city-state democracy. Nevertheless, they chose the practice of subsidiarity, i.e., subordination, but with decentralized and independent decision-making in defined societal areas, as in church hierarchy. The subsidiarity principle thus became the formula for the time's form of governance. Such is also the case in integrated Europe, which consists of almost ½ billion people and many different nations and government traditions.

Beyond this large and culturally integrated European political entity, comprehensive globalization processes and networking take place. Markets, institutions, and interests interact and coexist in non-transparent networks, global mutual dependence therefore arising, providing political opportunities for realization of common interests and also restrictions for national levels. It is said that a "global village" has been created, where everyone is more or less dependent on each other. According to a Norwegian impact study, there is a judicial-making of policy, to try to create a certain order[3] (Veggeland 2009). International agreements and regulations rather than direct political governance and democracy are used to create political

---

[3]The global financial crisis that began in 2008 demonstrates that such order is difficult to create. The problem of climate change is another example.

legitimacy, the regulatory state forms of governance being established according to the judicial-making of policies.

We can say that the new post-national democracy to a significant extent draws its legitimacy from three strategic choices.

- *Regulatory*: Develop and practice subsidiarity. The subsidiarity principle means that decisions are to be made at the lowest possible level in the EU system but high enough for the results to be effective. With the Lisbon Treaty, this becomes a legal principle in which violation of the principle can be appealed to the Court of Justice of the European Union. For the EEA countries of Norway and Iceland, this instance is the EFTA Court of Justice.
- *Economic*: The integrated territorial unit EU/EEA should prompt economic growth and stability nationally and competitiveness globally, i.e., create legitimacy by achieving results—"output"—in relation to given political goals.
- *Ideological*: By creating an increasingly public debate about the European entity's policy, more openness and transparency regarding economic and political processes is created, also by promoting liberal values in its culture building; see more on this below.

In short, the new post-national democracy has an enhanced potential for its citizens because it is geared toward achieving social, political, and economic results in a world of increasing interdependence between states, regions, and people. But "governance by the people" has increasingly become "governance for the people" through the judicial-making of policies (Scharpf 1999).

Nation Building and Democracy

The literature and our traditional view of representative democracy have been closely linked to the nation state and the emergence of what is commonly called the territorial state (Rokkan and Urwin 1983; Veggeland 2003). This is partly due to the fact that the formulas for such a type of democracy were designed by social thinkers and political scientists in parallel with the construction of the nation state in Europe.

As mentioned, the peace treaty signed in Westphalia in 1648 is considered to be the beginning of this process. As a rule of thumb, we can say that the "1500 politically and culturally unique entities that existed in the 16th century" came to be a result of these treaties, which were entered into between the great powers of the time. They merged into major territorial and political entities and constituted a strong central power, new borders being drawn and large territorial states becoming a fact. But the nation state, as we know it today, had to also be built culturally and politically, as did democracy. Several different national formulas were followed. Stein Rokkan (Rokkan and Urwin 1983), however, demonstrates, based on extensive European studies including Scandinavia, that a basic formula evolved in four phases.

According to Rokkan, the first phase of nation building begins with the establishment of a strong territorial power, which develops a hierarchy of institutions and bodies that govern and control the territory and its people. He calls this territorial consolidation. Max Weber (2000) emphasizes this by claiming that this power can be exercised in three terms: through physical power and force, through charismatic power,[4] or through legal power, i.e., legislation. The latter is fundamentally viewed as prominent in nation building.[5] But a problem arises. Who is to design the laws in a territory characterized by people representing varied histories, different cultures, traditions, and often different languages, composed of different nations and different identities? The answer came in the form of a functional law that muted internal conflicts. It was necessary not only to create a "demos" within the borders of the state, but also an "ethnos," that is, a unified people capable of communicating, who share common values and common goals for development.

Rokkan introduces the second phase of nation building, the phase of cultural consolidation. Building nationalism means emphasizing common historical roots and myths, creating a linguistic community through a comprehensive school and education system, creating common norms and values through enlightenment and learning, creating national literature and art,[6] gaining internal law enforcement, and habituating the population toward defense of national borders against foreign enemies. During this phase, the third phase could gradually begin.

In the third phase, according to Rokkan, the construction of representative democracy begins. National cultural community and identity make meaningful political discourse possible.

Parliamentary elections and suffrage legislation based on citizenship and requirements for citizenship are introduced. This creates the political involvement of the population, the constitution being the legal basis. Universal suffrage emerges over time, as enlightenment and citizen rights create a national community. If we take Norway as an example, only 7% of the citizens were granted suffrage in 1814, and it was only in 1913 that universal suffrage was passed in the Storting. With universal suffrage in the various nation states, the third phase ended with the establishment of mass democracy—this following two fundamentally different formulas.

In many European countries such as the Scandinavian ones, the consolidation of national identity was perceived as a done deal. These were therefore designated as "unitary states" and organized as territorial government hierarchies. In other countries, such as Germany, Austria, and Switzerland, this consolidation remained unfulfilled and was therefore organized as territorial "federal states," their distribution of power being stipulated by a constitution. This means that the legislative

---

[4]Charismatic power is exercised by personal projection and is the prerogative of persons in positions of power.

[5]The emergence of totalitarian national regimes since 1648 has certainly not been an unknown phenomenon in European nation building.

[6]In many countries in Europe, among them Norway, the period of the nineteenth-century national romance was very important in this context.

Table 5.1 Democracy was unequally designed during nation building with regard to the number of elected representatives and assemblies

Country	Number of citizens per elected representative	Average population per elected assembly
1. France (U)	116	1580
2. Germany (F)	250	4925
3. Italy (SF)	397	7130
4. Norway (U)	515	9000
5. Spain (SF)	597	4930
6. Sweden (U)	667	30,040
7. Denmark (U)	1084	18,760
8. United Kingdom (U)	2605	118,400

U unitary state, *F* federal state, *SF* semi-federal state

authority was divided between the central federal legislators and the legislatures in the states. In the unitary states, local democracy was also developed with elected political assemblies and local bureaucracy. Here, the national legislative authority was not, however, distributed. Local assemblies were granted power and duties on the basis of central political decisions. Authority was *delegated*. Delegation of authority means that this authority can, at any time, be formally withdrawn or amended by new central decisions. The local self-government of municipalities and regions in unitary states is therefore contingent, i.e., conditional, a form of governance practiced in, inter alia, Scandinavian countries.

However, in both unitary states and federal states, the organization of state, regional, and municipal democracy was often very different. In some states, the local units became numerous, as in the unitary state of France with its more than 36,000 municipalities and a corresponding number of elected representatives. There are far fewer, for example, in the Nordic countries, just a few hundred units. This can be illuminated by an overview prepared by the Council of Europe showing the situation in 1996 (with almost same numbers in 2018). Here, the *number of citizens per elected representative* is calculated, and the *average population per elected assembly* is calculated for a selection of European countries.

Table 5.1 shows the two clear extremes of France and the United Kingdom, both being unitary states (U), who have developed and chosen very different formulas for their democratic governance. France has a strong and large central state, but because of its many, small municipalities, the number of citizens behind each elected representative of a democratic assembly is small, the average population behind each elected assembly being correspondingly small. At the same time, it must be emphasized that the tasks the municipalities are responsible for are very varied, the many small municipalities in particular having a limited scope of authority. For example, Irish rural municipalities only have responsibility for local technical infrastructure, and this is also in close cooperation with the counties. Their most important task is to maintain the asphalt on all local roads so that they do not "wash away," much like the responsibility of Scandinavian municipalities before the 1960s (Amdam 1997).

Federal and semi-federal states (F and SF) also appear high in Table 5.1. This is due to the constitutional position of their member states. Semi-federal states delegate limited legislative authority to the regions and often have a large number of municipalities.

The United Kingdom is a centralized state. Government power is, however, limited in domestic affairs. Far fewer tasks and less political responsibility at the local and regional levels explain its position in the table. Here, public market actors such as unelected arm's-length organizations play a far more extensive role, which is in line with the country's Anglo-Saxon government tradition (Veggeland 2017). Consequently, local democracy plays a smaller role, and the average population per elected assembly is therefore correspondingly high.

According to Table 5.1, the Scandinavian countries, and especially Norway, rank high on the list. Despite a strong and large state, the significance of local democracy has grown due to extensive delegation of responsibility and authority. As shown above, the Scandinavian welfare states have used the municipalities as their most important welfare-producing instruments from the 1960s until today. Greater government requirements for quality and capacity push mergers or municipality cooperation. Today, in 2018, Denmark and Norway would also have exhibited significantly higher numbers in the two columns in Table 5.1, due to extensive merging of counties and municipalities in the middle of the 2000s. Sweden has considered and is considering also implementing this. The number of local governments has changed, and this matter is therefore an important element in the political debate in these countries. Obviously, the merging of municipalities is stimulated by the rise of the regulatory state order, which generates centralized decision-making. This also relates to phase four of nation building, at that time an unknown thought to Stein Rokkan.

According to Stein Rokkan's nation-building theory, the fourth phase came in the wake of mass democracy becoming a political reality. Political parties, NGOs, and voters demanded social equalization, equal distribution of resources socially and geographically, and, in line with prosperity development, more welfare for all. This required extensive central planning, sector planning. The development of the modern welfare state has taken place with strong legitimacy, in particular after World War II. The result was the central planned state and a phase of political stability and significant economic advancement for the many (Veggeland 2016).

The concept of democracy was therefore inextricably linked to the nation state through the four phases. The globalization process was, however, under way and with it the breakdown of traditional formulas of governance. The regulatory state was in the making, and with the rise of post-national democracy, new steering formulas were created. In the spirit of Rokkan, one can call this a fifth phase (Veggeland 2017).

The Post-National Democracy

Post-national democracy and its regulatory governance is, as we have seen, only to a limited extent based on the principles of the Keynesian central planning state. They are to a larger degree based on regulations, agreements, and partnerships negotiated in a multicentered, multilevel governance system. Constitutionally, there exists a critical relationship with the traditional doctrine of democratic order. This considers that the only form of democratic legitimacy is linked to democratic governance as being the basis for national power. "Democratic deficit" is used as a negative angle to the new forms of governance, both professionally and politically (Veggeland 2003; Kjær 2004). An alternative perspective is to look at post-national democracy as an order that holds potential in a globalized world, as one that promises more economic efficiency and new opportunities. Forms of governance are adapted to a time of weathering of the state and its traditional representative democracy, as Dahl (1989) claims. It is also expressed thus (Beetham and Lord 1998): "Democracy, after all, is not a matter of arrangements, but of effective popular agency." Let us take a closer look at this statement.

One can rightly claim that the political democratic governance in our part of the world, such as the Scandinavian countries, is increasingly emptied at all levels of decision-making in the form of direct political governance (OECD 2002, 2005). This has taken place in parallel with the historical emergence of the post-national state and along with the dwindling of the state's autonomy and transformation of its sovereignty. The intense increase of international interdependence in terms of technological and economic processes and activity, i.e., globalization and international integration, undermines the individual nation state's independent governance. Political internationalization with cross-border cooperation brings new arenas and new authorities at supranational levels. Tying this in to Stein Rokkan's four phases of nation building, it can be said that there is a deconsolidation of the territorial state. New identities develop across national borders, the national legislating authorities are weakened, and the conditions of the welfare state change (Iversen 2005). The nation state is still a central arena for political and economic transactions, but must find a new position in a system based on the organizational principle of multilevel governance, i.e., agreement-based multilevel governance.

The perception is that this multilevel governance system and agreements on sovereignty redistribution between nation states lead to a strongly increasing "democratic deficit" because the three liberal-democratic criteria for legitimizing authority, accountability, and representation have become unclear (Beetham and Lord 1998; Veggeland 2009). National democratic governance is emptied of its functions because decisions are increasingly rooted in national and international regulations, some by agreements, as is the case for example of EU and EEA member states. An important question is therefore: is this an undemocratic regime that is under political development or is this simply another form of democracy as promised by Robert A. Dahl (1989)? But, before answering these questions, let us examine the term "multilevel governance" and its meaning.

For a group of people living in a geographical area, say in a Norwegian county or city such as Oslo: how many legal authorities are authorized to exercise power over people living there at a given point in time? Through law enforcement, regulations, taxation, planning, development, financing, transport, education, social services, health care, and many more. Ten, a hundred, or a thousand legal authorities? These could be private actors or market actors governed by private law or corporate law, or they could be public actors governed by administrative law. They could be public actors, who, similar to private actors, are governed by corporate law or public special legislation because they have become organizationally "exempt" as market actors with a contractual service provider function. Examples of this include bus and ferry companies owned by county municipalities. They may also be principal authorities with the power to define goals for other businesses and with control and supervisory authority. Or they may be agents that are subordinate to the instructional authority of others. It was previously possible to imagine that authority was concentrated at the municipality, county, and state level and could be coordinated. Geographical and responsibility fragmentation has, however, created the need for new arenas, new forms of networking, and new forms of work and agreements (Amdam 2010).

Individuals, collectives, organizations, and institutions can be carriers of authority (Hooghe and Marks 2001). Some decision-makers could be locally based; others could be regionally, nationally, or internationally based. All authorities are subject to the Scandinavian countries' constitutions, with the exception of authorities that are anchored in international law and conventions that are superior to national law. Once upon a time in the childhood of nation building, it was said in Norway that "all power is gathered in this hall," i.e., the Storting. This was an expression of the prevailing perception of the nation state's monopoly of principal political power in this optimistic consolidation phase. Such a perception no longer applies, primarily due to globalization and the development of the networking community, this leading to political internationalization, i.e., the emergence of sovereignty distribution and multilevel governance agreements, as in the EU.

To count the sum total of authorities that are authorized at the various political levels, as Table1 shows, however, does not tell us how decision-making mandates and power are distributed between them (Hooghe and Marks 2001). One research strategy is to set up a list of policy areas and then evaluate how the authority over them is distributed. This is a strategy that is outlined in studies of power distribution in federal states, where the constitution fairly clearly defines the division of jurisdiction between the levels (Veggeland 2010a, b).

The strategy is also used in management studies of the decentralization of responsibility and tasks to municipalities and regions (Prud'homme 1995), and in studies of European integration and the relative role of the EU and national mandate (Deutsch et al. 1957; Schmitter 1996; Majone 1997; Scharpf 1999). However, this type of study is difficult to carry out when authorities and different decision-making skills overlap, i.e., by territorial integration and multilevel cooperation based on proceedings and regulations that interfere with each other.

Some types of expertise are, however, far more important than others. Constitutional authority, i.e., the authority to change formal and institutional norms and rules on how decisions are made, and to determine the agenda for important cases and issues, is fundamental to political governance. Unlike national unitary states where constitutional authority is monopolized by state power, this is distributed in federal states by constitutional provisions. The distribution of constitutional authorities in transnational multilevel governance is also not governed by a constitution that defines citizens' rights and obligations in relation to state power. Agreements and treaties govern the relationship between states, the separation of powers being subject to ever new negotiations and reallocations. They are legally valid until they may be renegotiated.

A particular issue arises in this context. This issue is that real legal agreements require, to be valid in relation to the law and democratic principles, at least two parties that are legal entities to take part in voluntary negotiations with a principal authority. In European integration, horizontal negotiations between independent member states are thus genuine, and agreements on intergovernmental cooperation, supra-nationality, and constitutional matters embodied in the many EU treaties are therefore valid and legal in both the legislative and democratic sense (Weiler 1999). What about vertical negotiations, negotiations between two principal authorities of the member state and the EU? Here national states sit on both sides of the table, and negotiations can hardly be said to be genuine in the legal sense, despite the fact that the democratic principles can be said to be observed (Beetham and Lord 1998: 25–29). It has been argued that good constitutional democratic practice in a Europe that is integrated through negotiation and agreement-based governance requires a federal EU to be further developed and that the EU must become a territorial state if this supranational level is to maintain legality and democratic legitimacy (Pindar 1993; Habermas 1996; Weiler 1999).

This reasoning on independent parties and on legal entities being a prerequisite for real legal and democratic negotiations also applies to self-determination based on subsidiarity and the decentralization of authority, as defined in terms of agreements and contracts. Traditional regionalized state authorities with delegated power, e.g., state agencies and administrative agencies, cannot conduct real negotiations and enter into legally binding agreements with the central authorities on the allocation of authority, tasks, and budgets. It is the political authorities that decide in such matters.

Negotiations should take place and agreements should be entered into between independent legal entities that are organized and have such a status of independence. From a decentralization perspective, there must be democratic authority at the local or regional level through a principal political mandate, or organizationally through independent regionalized enterprises and companies, i.e., self-regulating arm's-length bodies. Only then will the creation of arenas for the conclusion of legal agreements between levels and bodies that satisfy democratic principles in the modern regulatory state be possible.

This model involves the division of power between authorities at different levels. This is, even so, still different from the constitutional state order in federal European states. In these states, power distribution is constitutionally anchored. The model shares a greater affinity to that William Wallace (1998: 439) refers to as "Government without statehood: The unstable equilibrium." This is due to the principal authority of the parties being based on a negotiating mandate and entry into agreements and not on political delegation.

This leads to further questions that are important in terms of multilevel governance, i.e., the relationship between "multilevel governance" and democracy (Hooghe and Marks 2001).

- Do the authorities have a general or specialized mandate for the exercise of sovereignty?
- Does the authority of the individual actor apply to social areas that are mutually exclusive or overlapping?
- Is the authority's mandate unambiguously defined or flexible?
- Is the authority's mandate regulated through legislation or based on negotiations and changing agreements?

The answers to these questions are, with regard to the authority of the traditional unitary nation state, almost unambiguous. The state had a general mandate for the exercise of power and authority that was rooted in democratic governance, i.e., in the parliamentary decision-making chain. The state had exclusivity with regard to in which area of society it could exercise its legitimate power because, by definition, the nation state was equivalent to the territorial state and to a democracy, and because supranational international law enforced the principle of non-interventionism in national affairs. The state authority's mandate was unambiguously defined and constitutionally anchored. It was not based on changing negotiations and agreements. However, the answers become more complex for authority and multilevel governance. Lisbeth Hooghe and Gary Marks (2001), to clarify that multilevel governance and planning may have different characteristics, divide territorial authorities and post-national democracy into two main types. In our context, these main types can be related to the authority and governance of the two models on which the regulatory state is based on—the democratic model and the fragmentation model, as will be discussed in the next chapter.

Democracy and Central State Planning: Regulation and Complexity

"One can say that the planet and the factory are examples of closed systems. Complex systems, on the other hand, are open, dynamic and nonlinear, i.e. In such systems, small causes can have major consequences, and vice versa. Nonlinear systems can only be seen as totalities. They cannot be reduced to their constituent parts which, in turn, can be reassembled into a whole. They are 'inextricable'" (Nilsson and Uhlin 2002: 24).

Our focus is on theories of social governance and social planning, and we have presented a wide range of theories and perspectives to allow the reader to gain a deeper understanding, one that ultimately can be used to achieve better governance and planning. The different perspectives can be summed up as being founded on the differences between open and closed social systems and their respective perceptions of good governance and central state planning.

Control and a focus on function characterizes a closed system. The closed system can be divided into subsystems and their "building blocks," certain functions or roles being associated with each subsystem within the system as a whole. This can then be planned and managed separately, because of the unambiguous knowledge of the context in which it will work. Typical examples of such closed systems are a car or an instrument.

The system is composed of parts with different functions. All parts are, however, required for total functionality to be achieved. Changes in a subsystem can affect other subsystems and the system as a whole. These affects can, however, be predicted and compensated for by countermeasures. In principle, one has a complete overview of cause and effect, and how the subsystems are linked in a totality.

Based on this approach, complex situations in closed systems can be fragmented into smaller and more manageable subsystems and situations, which can be planned and managed individually because we believe we know the relationships of which they are a part. As in project planning, subprojects can be defined and assigned as specific groups. This approach is referred to below as the fragmentation model for post-national authority and governance, which corresponds to the instrumental models for public planning discussed in this chapter.

Open systems have a completely different character. They cannot be divided without losing something. Open systems are learning systems, dynamic, flexible, self-governing, nonlinear, and impossible to explain unambiguously. So, how can we handle them? There are two main directions within the attempts to develop public central planning theories for managing complex systems, as shown by Patsy Healey (2010).

- The instrumental (fragmented) approach rests on the assumption that complex systems can be "mathematically" modeled (if enough research funds are available) and can be controlled through the influence of parameters in the model. Models can be used to simulate results of different types of regulations and measures. This approach is reflected in policy analysis and "comprehensive planning" (Healey 1993). Such planning models have a clear "outside perspective" on systems and, as we claim here, cannot work in high complexity cases. Regulatory state governance in particular, with its hard regulations, has a strong affinity to this thinking model. Governing actors often, in practice, become instrumentally delimited or have to use a pragmatic grip, muddling through, because the models and measures they prescribe do not produce the desired effects (Amdam and Veggeland 1998; Amdam and Amdam 2000).
- The communicative (democratic) approach, in which the fundamental complexity is also related to a lack of information and communication. Actors in a complex dynamic system cannot have a full overview of their own situation or environment because these are constantly changing. Through conversations, trust building, networking, and shared learning, the system and actors can act selectively

and reduce the complexity for themselves within the system through organization and collaboration. An example of this is the development of institutions, organizations, and also "game rules" as norms and values for interaction, trust, and mutual learning (Healey 1997, 2007; Forester 1986, 1993). The four phases of Rokkan in democracy and nation building, as presented previously, are examples of such processes.

The instrumental approach requires external control by means of hard regulation and is well suited to the regulatory state order. The communicative approach is, however, characterized by those who attempt to govern, having to participate in the same way as those who are to be governed (in a communicative soft regulated community) in democratic processes and bodies. As Nilsson and Uhlin (2002) point out, this is the basis for newer national and regional development models such as Triple Helix and Cluster Theory (Porter 1990; Storper 1997), in which soft regulations are in focus. There are clear links between planning theory, regional development theories, and democratic governance theories. We therefore, as noted, present two main types of governance models for examining the links between multilevel governance and social planning.

Type I: Democratic Model for Post-National Authority and Governance
The historical model of governance that forms the basis for the type I model formula for organization is constitutional federalism, as formed in the construction of the nation state. The democratic federal state is based on the division of power between a limited number of territorial authorities based in democratic governance and with a correspondingly small number of levels each with a degree of difference in terms of their identity. The organization is vertical, a central authority balancing its power in relation to subnational democratic levels. Regulatory measures are at this stage.

Summarizing, there are constitutionally assigned authorities that do not generally overlap territorially or by sectors. The complex total system is divided into geographically defined entities that are still complex but more transparent. At the same time, this may cause coordination problems both in relation to the smaller and to the larger democratic systems.

The political authority at each level has an extensive but limited mandate, which is legally and politically legitimate and linked to defined areas of responsibility such as land use, infrastructure, education, and basic welfare. This decision-making mandate can apply to culture, economics, and politics. The levels are, at the same time, responsible for coordinating public planning, development and financial initiatives, and national allocation policy. The authorities' mandate is stable and lasting over time, precisely because it is constitutional. Its mandate has not been obtained on the basis of historical chance negotiations between the levels, subsequently settled through an agreement.

Legislation today in Norwegian social planning has such a character that the municipalities and counties have a relatively clearly defined delegated authority, in relation to both social development and area planning (Kleven 2011). This differs from the statutory provisions on regional and district planning in the 1965 legislation. These plans were not unambiguously linked to democratic entities and governing bodies, but were based on a presupposed cooperation and understanding between several municipalities or county councils or a state "override." A clear weakness is that this planning and governing authority is not constitutionally anchored, but delegated from the state through provisions in the planning legislation, provisions that can easily be changed. The authority is also not superior. State sectoral authorities have opposition rights within many decision-making areas, which means that decisions can be transferred to higher (state) levels.

The division of sovereignty between political levels is thus a characteristic aspect of democratic federalism and differs from multilevel governance in unitary states. It also differs from multilevel governance in the EU system that Scandinavian countries are affiliated to through the EU and EEA Agreements. The difference is clear, this difference according to William Wallace's view (Wallace 1998) being related to the lack of traditional "statehood" in the supranational and regional level within multilevel governance. It is true that, in this case, there is also a transfer, even devolution, and distribution of sovereignty and authority from the democratic national level both up to the supranational regulatory EU level and down to national, regional, and municipal levels in the top-down regulatory system. This implies that this redistribution is rooted in treaties and agreements that regulate the relationship between member states and the EU and not in a constitutional hierarchy.[7]

The national parliaments, as representatives of the nation states, are given both an independent negotiating mandate and a decision-making mandate in the negotiation of and in the settlement of agreements. This does mean that the traditional state instructional authority is, on the one hand, transferred to both supranational and regional parliaments, but on the other hand also to comprehensive agreements, which are adopted on the basis of a consensus on "distribution of governance" (OECD 2002). These agreements represent a legal authority in relation to the levels, they having their own legal instructional power and governance functions vis-à-vis the supranational cooperative institutions, and correspondingly the regional and local planning and development institutions and other bodies.

According to the democratic model, the supranational EU level principally only "recognizes" the nation state powers as authorities and counterparts.[8] Subnational authorities can directly negotiate with the EU for participation in, for example, various development programs such as "Interreg" regional development programs or education or research programs. However, for constitutional reasons, state power in decisions is exclusive and superior. On the other hand, as mentioned above, the mandate of the supranational EU is largely linked to the regulation and development of development programs, while the national level is the main actor in terms of distribution policy and sectoral policy. The mandate regarding the organization of public management and administration is also exclusively national, the EU having no legal interference rights.

---

[7]In the mid-2000s, the EU tried to adopt a "Constitution Treaty," but France and the Netherlands voted against it following referendums.

[8]For some member states in federal states, exceptions are made for constitutional reasons.

The post-national democratic model linked to the regulatory state multilevel governance form may otherwise be described through the following characteristic features.

- Following the democratic model for multilevel governance, efforts are made to make political mandate mutually exclusive in line with the principle of subsidiarity, as enshrined in the Maastricht and Lisbon treaties. Political decisions must be made by elected representatives at the lowest possible level, yet high enough to achieve effectiveness and results.
- The distribution of authority is, likewise, stable in the sense that it is rooted in treaties, agreements, and programs, in addition to territorial democracy and thus in the clear administrative units and delimited jurisdictions that ensure that overview is not lost.
- The authorities' mandate is furthermore linked to communicative planning and action (Healey 2010), as it presupposes negotiation arenas and builds on the "mutuality principle" as set out in the Maastricht Treaty. Individual legal entities are a prerequisite for actions. This entails interactive communication between independent political parties, and therefore the establishment of legal agreements and the distribution of tasks between levels according to democratic principles.

Multilevel governance following the democratic model is not limited to constitutional federal states such as Germany, Austria, Switzerland, and Belgium. On the contrary, studies show that such governance is widespread: "The decision-making process evolving in the Community gives key role to governments—national government at the moment, and [...] subnational governments increasingly in selected arenas" (Sbragia 1992: 289).

Lisbeth Hooghe and Gary Marks (2001: 2) support this perception, but the end of the following quote should be noted: "[...] polity-creating processes in which authority and policy-making influence are shared across multiple levels of government—subnational, national, and supranational. *While national governments (remain) formidable participants in EU policy making, control has slipped away from them.*"

The end of the quote refers to a more problematic side of contemporary multilevel governance, namely the metamorphosis which democratic governance has been subject to. Elected assemblies at different levels have lost overview and control. This is linked to another multilevel governance model that has expanded since the 1980s.

Type II: The Fragmentation Model for Post-National Authority and Regulatory Governance

An alternative model to multilevel governance is one in which the number of independent legal entities, both territorial and sectoral authorities, significantly increases. The political result is a large number of authorities of different characteristics, rather than relatively few and transparent ones described as Type I. In the model for post-national type II authority and governance, which follows the fragmentation model, the authorities are economically and functionally specialized and operate on many levels and within overlapping jurisdictions, which follows an NPM model. The fragmentation model is intended to create flexible multilevel governance and to unlock the predicted power of state bureaucracy and the planned state's direct political governance. It thus represents the regulatory state's mode of governance in a post-national and transnational context. The democratic model strives for a coordinated (political) territorial planning (comprehensive). It is, however, usually vertical top-down coordination that is the focus of the fragmentation model in terms of sectors (Amdam and Amdam 2000).

The vision behind the model has a market-liberal perspective as its starting point, this including a desire for minimization of the state and the marketing of the emerging national hierarchy, including the EU hierarchy. The model is based on NPM's principles of an economically efficient form of governance, which also applies to separation and specialization for post-national development. The preferences of the model are often supported by neoclassical economists and likewise by social theorists. Their preference is rational choice theories in political science or instrumental (evidence-based) forms of planning and hard regulation.

Authorities are, in the fragmentation social model, made into actors that are not territorially exclusive, but perform their functions in often overlapping competing jurisdictions and at different levels. As Alessandra Casella and Barry Weingast write (1995: 13): "There is generally no reason why the smaller jurisdictions should be neatly contained within the borders of the larger ones. On the contrary, borders will be crossed, and jurisdictions will partly overlap. The 'nested', hierarchical structure of the nation-state has obvious rationale and is opposed by economic forces" (Casella and Weingast 1995: 13).

National and transnational authorities grow as enterprises and companies, private and public, each with added specific functions. Their constitutional independence entails that they are organizationally self-regulating as market actors and independent of national borders. They may be service providers, regional development actors, or financial operators. Theoretically they are flexibly specialized and customer-oriented market actors, operating in a globalized network economy, this being described as being post-fordism as opposed to oligarchic activity with few major actors (Amin 1994). They are trading legal entities who compete in a post-national territorial space.

The fragmentation model is therefore characterized by specialized and geographical authorities, which are outlined as overlapping authorities. Which level should be the principal authority and hold the mandate as regulator of the many policy areas is, however, a political point of conflict in the EU's supranational and intergovernmental cooperation. The conflict centers on which mandate should belong to the EU institutions, the national state power or the regional political authorities. The conflict is also based on another dimension that relates to the relationship with marketized public actors, with arm's-length agencies (PLAs and PLBs), and with private actors. Such hybrid self-regulatory actors have grown in number and are made up of enterprises, companies, bodies, financial institutions, and NGOs.

The fragmentation model has also created supervisory and control institutions as part of the regulatory state, which have a mandate to both approve and test product standards and quality, health standards, and safety and environmental standards. They have exploded in numbers in most European countries since the 1980s (Majone 1997). These institutions include competition authorities, credit supervision, health oversight, vehicle inspection, labor inspection, and similar institutions in various other areas of society. ESA, the EFTA Surveillance Authority, also belongs to this category, the ESA having authority over EFTA countries in the EEA cooperation. In Norway, we are familiar with the so-called EEA inspection of cars every 2 years. Private car workshops have also been authorized to carry out this inspection in Norway.

The upward trend is linked to the development of the EU as an increasingly comprehensive regulatory authority and the implementation and monitoring of international agreements and conventions. The setting of standards and the associated surveillance authorities are in general knowledge-based, because of the specialization this represents in relation to tasks. They authorities are organized as arm's-length bodies from public administration, with a high degree of autonomy and with overlapping authority.

Multilevel governance is, following the fragmentation model, ubiquitous and works in parallel with the democratic model, i.e., in which vertically organized authorities are weak (Rosenau 1997). In the regulatory state, this has created two different ways of interpreting and implementing the governance formula set out by the EU's subsidiarity principle. In professional terminology and politics, it is equally popular to talk about "outward devolution" as "downward devolution," i.e., "beyond" decentralization and the transfer of power and authority, and as a transfer through decentralization "downward" in political-administrative significance. This interpretation has been particularly prominent in Anglo-Saxon countries, but it has also entered the Nordic model. This involves organizing independent legal entities and self-regulation, these no longer only applying to the private sector but also now to the public sector. It is no longer the case that elected representatives are the only principal political and regulatory authorities. Now a variety of other hybrid authorities operate in post-national society within national and international borders (Veggeland 2010a, b).

Studies of consequences show that opacity is a facet of the fragmentation model, which negatively affects the governance potential and causes, inter alia, limited stability in terms of which mandate is assigned to which instance in each case (OECD 2002). For example, between 1970 and 2000 more than 150 international environmental and climate policy agreements were entered into and signed between authorities, so making this area highly complex. This number has further increased, and these agreements are for a social area. Who monitors and interprets national and EU law? A democratic deficit is therefore created in this way when based on a traditional definition of democracy.

Conflicts between sectoral planning, which are usually anchored in special legislation, and attempts at territorial democratic coordination are also demonstrable in Scandinavian social planning. Kleven (2011) points out that while weak authorities and actors try to be enrolled as partners in planning legislation to ensure access to local and regional planning processes, powerful actors try to avoid a corresponding position. The powerful actors have the power to "drive over" or "outside" local municipal and county planning processes, which must therefore largely be adapted to such sector plans. In the work on the development of special area and in building central state planning, there have also been many initiatives that have attempted to break the territorial, democratic governance principles embodied in the democratic tradition. There is a political will to replace them with legislation and regulatory measures adapted to the fragmentation model and NPM, for example, in connection with the latest legislation amendment (Kleven 2011).

The idea and the rationale behind the fragmentation model for post-national public authority is derived from specialized private organization, referred to as post-fordism. Post-fordism is reflected in the organization of multilevel governance. This, however, requires the coordination of the many authorities and the setting of goals for their operation, especially when cooperation is required. One strategy to counter this is the organization of public–public or public–private partnerships (Higdem 2007). This is characteristic of all European cross-border and cross-level cooperation of programs and development plans such as cross-border cooperation (Interreg. EU programs), urban cooperation (Urban EU Program), the police (Schengen), immigration, culture, education, research, and climate. Cooperation also takes place at the national and regional level. One can argue that Anglo-Saxon communicative planning has, in particular, been developed to create soft regulatory processes and arenas for the development of such cooperation and partnerships (Allmendinger 2009: 218).

The following examples can be given for Scandinavia that are related to attempts to counteract the negative effects of fragmentation, examples including the so-called Regional Development Plans. These plans are based on negotiated partnerships between the counties and regional government agencies. The attempted "unitary county" as a partnership between regional political authorities and regionalized state enterprises is outlined in White Paper No. 19 (2001–2002). "Cooperative municipalities" are a partnership between municipalities on service production and tasks; programs that require the participation of various cooperative institutions, such as research programs; the establishment of network centers and coordinating responsibility in the areas of authority, innovation and culture, etc.; and forms for negotiation planning in connection with area planning in complex ownership and interest conditions. To a large extent such partnerships in a Norwegian context are attempts to counteract public fragmentation.

The post-national fragmentation model can be briefly described with the following characteristic features:

The fragmentation model for multilevel governance contains no aim to make the political mandate mutually exclusive and linked to elected representatives at the various levels. The principle of subsidiarity, as laid down in the Maastricht Treaty, is interpreted as a formula for both downward transfer of power and authority in the hierarchy and to the public authorization of hybrid arm's-length bodies.

The distribution of the authority of the regulatory state is unrealistic and unstable in the sense that it is strongly rooted in self-regulatory institutions, bodies, and partnerships. Overlapping authority and jurisdiction also play a role in this.

The authorities' mandate is not primarily related to communicative planning and action, because it is largely based on hybrid self-regulatory public and private actors. Individual legal entities are a prerequisite for actions. However, the introduction of the partnership concept with prior negotiations somewhat counteracts this, but not in a democratic sense.

The authority is founded in a technocratic way, as it is anchored in expert bodies exercising authority on the basis of specialized knowledge related to hard regulation and technical rationality. The legitimacy of the form of governance that follows the fragmentation model been referred to as "a technocratic version" of legitimacy, a functional legitimacy because it works in its context (Beetham and Lord 1998: 16).

Post-national multilevel regulatory governance following the fragmentation model is closely linked to the Anglo-Saxon formula for governance and has become part of the EU/EEA structure. International network organizations generally follow the model to a greater or lesser extent. However, "while governments can rarely if ever perform any function that a non-governmental institution cannot also perform, government of a function—that is, passing a public policy—is sought because the legitimacy of its sanctions makes social controls more surely effective" (Lowi 1992: 37).

Decision-making processes will, with an increasing number of actors in the post-national governance system, become increasingly time-consuming, the ability to identify political responsibility will decrease, and the experience of commitment by the individual actor will be weakened. Efficiency decreases and crises have been proven to be due to inadequate coordination and regulation. One example is the financial crisis that "unexpectedly" occurred in 2008 as a result of the many uncoordinated transactions and actors, over which no one had any overview, and therefore no regulation. As G. Majone (1997: 267–268) writes: *"current economic, political and technological developments tend to reduce drastically the effectiveness, and thus erode also the legitimacy, of coercive policy instruments. A particularly important development is the increasing openness of national borders."* Post-national state building faces other challenges than those faced by national state building, as Stein Rokkan has shown in his work.

The New Democracy and Its Lack of Legitimacy

We have a public expectation, based on traditional perception and democratic theory, that decision-makers as people's representatives are appointed on the basis of free constitutional democratic elections (Beetham and Lord 1998: 22). When this perception is not adhered to, as in the case of governance following the fragmentation model, then a democracy and legitimacy problem is created. This problem is indicated by inadequate political support and participation in elections by citizens, or skeptical attitudes in general toward political authorities, as expressed in opinion polls. In Europe, as in Norway, it is not uncommon for the legitimacy problem to be linked to the previously mentioned democratic deficit.

The democratic deficit is often analyzed in connection with European integration because the EU, as a supranational uniting body, operates and exerts power explicitly through a set of treaties and agreements as a basis for governance. Moreover, the European Union has a complex and hard-to-follow institutional decision-making system.

This system achieves a number of desired results that provide output legitimacy. It does not, however, satisfy liberal, democratic principles of openness, publicity, and transparency, i.e., the conditions for broad popular discourse on goals, measures, and development. The latest power and democracy investigation claims that Norway, with its EEA association, further reinforces the EU-created democratic deficit. This is the case in a double sense: firstly, because of integration into the EU system, and secondly because Norway is not a member state with the right and duty to participate in the political processes of the Union. This is correct in and of itself. This perspective on the democratic deficit in the EU system is, however, too narrow and partly misleading. For example, a political conclusion from this point of view could be that the democratic deficit is a consequence of European integration. This is, of course, a misinterpretation.

Democratic deficits have a far-reaching definition and must be seen in the context of how governance in the regulatory state is implemented according to the democratic model and fragmentation model and which of the models is emphasized. There is imbalance between these models, not only in the EU but also in the individual member states and in Norway.

Complexity, Democracy, and Planning

At the national level, as in Norway, the balance between the two types of legitimacy is in better shape than in the EU system. The input legitimacy and the institutions it rests on are preserved and the parliamentary decision chain is intact. However, as we have seen, the field of its influence has been significantly reduced. Post-national governance, following the fragmentation form, has been added. A simple four-field table shows the relationship between the democratic model and the fragmentation model described above, as formulas for governance, and their shifting legitimacy.

Let us look into the model in Table 5.2. Criteria that, according to the democratic model, normally form the basis of legitimacy and are referred to in the literature as

Table 5.2 Democratic deficit linked to legitimacy

	Input legitimacy	Output legitimacy
Nationally		
Democratic model	High	Low
Post-nationally		
Fragmentation model	Low	Moderate

"input" legitimacy consist of a number of elements (Scharpf 1999; Weiler 1999; Veggeland 2003).

Input Legitimacy

(A) Legality: The authorities subordinate and exercise power in accordance with elections and with other established constitutional laws, regulations, and norms.

(B) Normativity: The legitimacy of the authorities is consistent with the social and cultural perceptions of the citizens in regard to goals and standards of governance and the order that authorization follows.

(C) Efficiency: Decisions taken in elected assemblies must function properly and be implemented by bureaucracy that is neutral and loyal to policy makers.

(D) Publicity: The authority's positions of power have been confirmed by publicly expressed support from the citizens, approval by subordinate actors, and acknowledgment from internationally legitimate state powers.

It is a common belief that the democratic model is stronger on "input" legitimacy than the fragmentation model. Criteria that normally form the basis of legitimacy, following the fragmentation model, are commonly referred to as "output" legitimacy. These criteria also consist of a number of elements (Beetham and Lord 1998; Scharpf 1999; Veggeland 2003).

Output Legitimacy

(E) *Openness and transparency* at all levels, in all processes, and also when self-regulation occurs.

(F) *Informative management* and personal responsibility. Publicity and involvement of citizens and civil society.

(G) *Post-national subsidiarity* and the practice of multilevel governance based on the democratic model.

(H) *Results* as the consequence of regulation, prioritizing problems and solution options.

(I) *Rights regulation* based on international law's post-national order.

In simple terms, we can say that input legitimacy of democracy is created based on the parliamentary decision chain, a constitution, rule of law, and democratic electoral schemes. The principle of legality requires authority to be exercised in accordance with the identity, values, and objectives of the national community, that minority groups' rights are accepted and respected, and that political authority has a mandate from the people. Power positions, such as government power, depend on and are confirmed by majority voting. They change when the necessary support expires, and national sovereignty is legitimized through the recognition of other international sovereign states. Fritz Scharpf (1999: 6) calls this "governance by the people" and these are also fundamental principles in, for example, the Planning and Building Act with certain limitations (Kleven 2011).

The legitimacy problem of national democracy, i.e., its input legitimacy crisis, was mentioned by Jürgen Habermas as early as the 1970–1980s (1987). Today, it appears primarily in relation to point C in the above list, i.e., in relation to the efficiency criterion. Globalization processes and the internationalization of markets, with the resulting uncontrolled financial flows and multinational corporations, have created economic crises such as the stagflation crisis and the financial crisis in the 2000s, in addition to environmental and climate problems, food crises, migration problems, and cross-border crime. These are issues that cannot be solved nationally. National and international regulation, combined with agreements and controls, must be implemented as countermeasures. At the same time, a larger number of self-regulating public actors should be put in operation. In short, there are new formulas for post-national problem solving following the fragmentation model.

The model solves some problems and achieves results that cannot be achieved by individual states. However, according to Fritz Scharpf (1999: 6), the model entails "governance for the people." Such a form of governance also requires legitimacy in relation to the "people" that "it governs." Output legitimacy is required, which is not just anchored in the results and innovations that are created and the problem-solving that can be documented, point (H) above, but other criteria, (E) to (I), must also be met. These are all liberal democratic criteria that ideally should characterize an "open society" with an informed opinion. This means that social processes are open and transparent, that the flow of information reaches the people, that authorities' responsibility is clearly divided, that decisions are made at the lowest possible democratic level in line with the subsidiarity principle, and that fundamental rights are ensured in accordance with international law.

The post-national EU regulatory system fails in a democratic sense, particularly with regard to legitimacy criteria (E) to (G), and as expressed in the dissatisfaction detected in many opinion polls. Popular criticism of the EU as an elite-controlled and closed system is widespread and still current. Reforms are required to improve output legitimacy, and there is still a need for reform aimed at strengthening the parliamentary bodies in the Union, i.e., strengthening input legitimacy, a long-term process (Wallace et al. 2005). The democratic deficit therefore has a dual character, one characterized by inadequate input and output legitimacy while also lacking democratic institutions.

Similar challenges are seen at local and regional levels in today's Norway. Municipalities and counties have, in the postwar period, changed their role from being local and regional development and politicizing organizations chosen by and for the people, into executives of government policy. State decrees and statutory rights limit the political authorities' planning and action areas, for example, in developing multisectoral solutions adapted to local conditions. Instead, they must adapt their activities to the principles of the fragmentation model.

Multilevel governance in Europe and Scandinavia must be considered to be a political attempt to emerge from a national decision-making crisis, by regaining post-national legitimacy through increased market efficiency, macroeconomic stabilization, and measures for social and economic cohesion. This is achieved through establishing a new political order, an output democratic order, which achieves legitimacy, primarily through showing results in relation to the challenges and problems of our time. This legitimacy is, however, of a different nature from the democratic legitimacy created by historic nation building (Beetham and Lord 1998: 16). It is problematic, because it has so far not been closely linked to the universal liberal, democratic criteria.

This also represents a fundamental challenge for social planning, a challenge that is largely solved in the prevailing planning theories presented below. Healey (1997, 2007), for example, points to many sensible demands for good communicative planning, but still has a "dissolving" discussion on democracy and social governance (Healey 2007). Point to three main elements in their argumentation for communicative planning in cases of high complexity. These are not particularly developed democratically but are mostly focused on the challenges created by the fragmentation model.

Joint Learning and Task Resolution

Communicative processes designed and directed to generate collaborative rationality will be able to produce effective opportunities for actors to work with and solve their common problems. Individual and collective learning that also make society and social networks more adaptable and development-oriented can be promoted. This means that the actors and the system that adapt to regulations through common and individual learning put in place countermeasures or unintended practices that can mean that the results of regulations can be completely different than intended, or that they manifest differently in different systems and situations. For example, the Norwegian hospital sector is divided into four area-based enterprises. It is therefore likely that the same national rules and incentives will lead to a number of different measures and implementations in the different regions, because enterprises and regions face different situations and challenges. Rules and regulations that can work well in one situation can be meaningless in another. This is because the challenges and problems they are prepared to solve are often complex and hard to follow and can be interpreted very differently. These can be called "wicked problems." "Wicked problems" do not have optimal solutions, and they therefore cannot be handled instrumentally (evidence-based). The communicative process and dialogue can therefore cause the actors to work together to improve their own situation, instead of searching for "the best" or the most "just" solution seen from the regulatory state's perspective. Break away, privatization, minimization of public direct governance, and formalization of self-governance can and will just cause organizations to "optimize" their own benefit or long-term survival, based on their own learning. They would like to push "wicked problems" on to others, instead of acting as expected by regulatory authorities. This can lead to societal challenges and to tasks that provide income and status to attract competition. An attempt is also made to hide or "delegate" onward to others; government agencies "delegate problems" to municipalities or independent governmental organizations.

Process Organization Based on the Requirement for Soft Communicative Action

It is very important to know how collaborative processes work and evolve over time in complex systems. It is not enough to gather actors for joint meetings on the issues, procedures, solutions, and working methods of the processes. This interaction does not meet the basic requirement for communicative rationality. Complex systems are largely self-governing and self-organizing. Key actors in key change processes will therefore assess the benefits to themselves of participating in the short and long term. They may be commanded to participate. They then usually participate to control processes, the aim being to minimize harm to themselves. Process design, for example, in the development of soft regulations, cooperation, and partnerships, is therefore very important and must be developed in accordance with the special circumstances and in such a way that all key actors have a say in them and benefit from participation. In fact, it is problematic to develop "formulas" that are in addition to general requirements, because the processes and communication must be tailored and continuously adapted to actual circumstances. In fact, this requires processes to demonstrate the same type of development that call institutional capital in the form of linking knowledge resources, network resources, and mobilization capabilities, i.e., the ability to face "wicked problems" and other common challenges.

System Changes

Also argues that collaborative processes can lead to changes in the overreaching systems. The institutions we have, including both the hard and soft regulations, the statutory and the practiced, can be more efficient and adaptable, because the participants in the communicative processes will bring experiences to other venues and processes and promote collaborations there. Participants gain new and deeper knowledge and learn new skills, for example on how to organize communicative, development-oriented meetings in complex systems. They also gain access to new networks, professional as well as social, and develop norms and values through co-learning and, for such reasons, ask questions about "adopted truths" and established practice. Actors change behavior through such co-learning processes. They organize and collaborate in new ways that change the complex system.

That which Healey, to a limited extent, focuses on in the theoretical review and choice of examples is the importance of *democratic legitimacy* and the central role that democratic bodies should play, particularly because such collaborative planning can be instrumental in both democratic and fragmented governance. Collaborative planning that focuses on fragmented challenges does not have the legitimacy of democratic bodies and of real collaborations of all legitimate and real interests. This type of planning can therefore reinforce fragmentation in society instead of promoting democratic legitimacy. It can therefore, based on this, be argued that communicative planning is more an attempt to respond to postmodern society's fragmentation challenges than an attempt to provide models for the further development of planning that are based on the democratic model. For example, Allmendinger (2009: 212) points out that collaborative planning, to a too limited extent, acts as a counterpart to fragmented planning and that power relations are, to a too limited extent, in focus. This is a criticism argues against in a newly written Chap. 10 of the latest edition.

A basic perception in postmodern thinking and also in postmodern planning is that every situation, case, and challenge is special and must be solved on the basis of its special features (Allmendinger 2009). Processes must therefore be planned and organized based on the particular circumstances of the particular case. Experience from earlier processes and solutions can be built upon, to some extent (neopragmatism). These must, however, critically adapt to new situations in active discourse with the participants.

What we have tried to show is that complexity theory can answer why the regulatory state's and fragmentation model's grip does not work democratically in complex systems. A "Regulatory Explosion" of ever new and necessarily more detailed regulations can be the result of attempting to meet such challenges, regulations that lead to the need for new regulations to counteract unintended effects. Veggeland (2009, 2010a, b) does not use complexity theory in his analysis. All of his analysis and results, however, indicate developmental features that can be expected from complexity theory. Open systems are dynamic, nonlinear, self-regulating, and self-organizing and no system and subsystem are therefore alike. Regulations and fragmented planning will therefore yield different results in different situations. Social planning must also change character, must be less dependent on "formulas," and must be more focused on current challenges and on democratic input and output legitimacy. Perhaps, as Allmendinger (2009: 217 our translation) argues with a certain foundation in Healey (1997), what we have left is a hint of how planning and governance can work in complex democratic societies following this manifest.

- Planning should use all types of techniques and forms of presentation. Aside from the current situation, there is no "universal formula" or theory.
- Common languages cannot be developed between discourse communities. Planning must therefore focus on and search for possible higher levels of common understanding.
- Planning should facilitate respectful discussion within and between discourse communities.

- Planning should involve the construction of arenas where processes are developed and formulated and conflicts identified.
- All forms of knowledge and rationality are allowed.
- Reflective and critical capacity must be maintained through the use of "ideal conversation."
- Everyone with an interest is included (or at least not excluded). Dilemma must be almost "interdiscursive."
- Interests are not stable and final. People will change interests through interaction and mutual learning.
- It is possible to change existing power structures through criticism and by emphasizing repressive and dominant powers.
- The goal is to help planners (democratic bodies, politicians, leaders) to work in ways that are generally acceptable and based on interdiscursive understanding.

In addition, we also emphasize:

- Planning must, through theory and method development and in practice, strengthen democratic work and democratic institutions to achieve the highest possible input and output legitimacy in society.
- This can be achieved by strengthening the work by further developing governance models and community planning within the framework of the democratic model and by counteracting fragmentation and regulation explosion.

References

Allmendinger, P. (2009, 2002). *Planning theory*. Basingstoke: Palgrave Macmillan.

Amdam, J. (1997). Planning for rural and local development in Ireland and Norway. In R. Byron, J. Walsh, & P. Breathnach (Eds.), *Sustainable development on the North Atlantic margin*. Aldershot: Ashgate.

Amdam, J., & Amdam, R. (2000). *Kommunikativ planlegging*. Oslo: Det norske samlaget.

Amdam, J., & Veggeland, N. (1998). *Teorier om samfunnsplanlegging*. Oslo: Universitetsforlaget.

Amdam, R. (2010). *Planning in health promotion work: An empowerment model*. Abingdon: Routledge.

Amin, A. (Ed.). (1994). *Post-fordism*. Oxford-Cambridge: Blackwell.

Bachrach, P., & Baratz, M. S. (1972). *Power and poverty: Theory and practice*. New York: Oxford University Press.

Beetham, D., & Lord, C. (1998). *Legitimacy and the European Union*. Kondon-New York: Longman.

Casella, A., & Weingast, B. R. (1995). Elements of a theory of jurisdictional change. In B. Eichengreen et al. (Eds.), *Politics and institutions in an integrated Europe*. New York-Heidelberg: Springer.

Dahl, R. A. (1989). *Who governs? Democracy and power in an American City*. New Haven, CT: Yale University Press.

Deutsch, K. W., Burrell, S. A., Kann, R. A., Lee, M., Lichterman, M., Raymond, E., et al. (1957). *Political community and the North Atlantic Area: International organization in the light of historical experience*. Princeton: Princeton University Press.

Forester, J. (1986). *Planning in the face of power*. Berkeley, CA: University of California Press.

Forester, J. (1993). *Critical theory, public policy and planning practice: Toward a critical pragmatism*. Albany, NY: University of New York Press.

Habermas, J. (1987). *The theory of communicative action*. Cambridge, MA: Polity Press.

Habermas, J. (1996). Why Europe needs a constitution. In R. Rogowski & C. Turner (Eds.), *The shape of the New Europe*. Cambridge: Cambridge University Press.

Healey, P. (1993). The communicative turn in planning theory. In E. Fisher & J. Forester (Eds.), *The argumantative turn in policy analysis and planning*. Durham, London: Duke University Press.

Healey, P. (2006, 1997). *Collaborative planning. Shaping places in fragmented societies*. Basingstoke: Palgrave Macmillan.

Healey, P. (2007). *Urban complexity and spatial strategies. Toward a relational planning for our times. The RTPI Library Series*. London: Routledge.

Healey, P. (2010). *Making better places. The planning project in the twenty-first century*. Hampshire: Palgrave Macmillan.

Higdem, U. (2007). *Regional partnerships and their constructions and implementations: A case study of the counties of Oppland, Hedmark, and Østfold*. Ås, Norway: UBM.

Hooghe, L., & Marks, G. (2001). Types of multi-level governance. *European Integration Online Papers, 5*(11), 32.

Innes, J. E., & Booher, D. E. (2010). *Planning with complexity. An introduction to collaborative rationality for public policy*. London and New York: Routledge.

Iversen, T. (2005). *Capitalism, democracy and welfare*. Cambridge: Cambridge University Press.

Kjær, A. M. (2004). *Governance*. Cambridge, MA: Polity Press.

Kleven, T. (2011). *Fra gjenreisning til samfunnsplanlegging. Norsk kommuneplanlegging 1965–2005*. Trondheim: Tapir akademisk forlag.

Lowi, T. (1992). *The state of political science: How we became what we study. American Political Science Review, 86, 82–101*.

Majone, G. (1997). From the positive to the regulatory state: Causes and consequences of change in the mode of government. *Journal of Public Policy, 17*(3), 139–189.

Nilsson, J. E., & Uhlin, Å. (2002). *Regionala innovasjonssystem. En fordjupad kunnskapsøversikt*. Stockholm: Vinnova.

OECD. (2002). *Distributed public governance: Agencies, authorities and other government bodies*. Paris: OECD.

OECD. (2005). *Modernising government: The way forward*. Paris: OECD.

Olsen, J. P. (red). (1978). *Politisk organisering*. Oslo.

Olsen, J. P. (red). (1980). *Meninger om makt*. Oslo.

Pindar, J. (1993). *The new European federalism: The idea and the achievement*. New York-London: Harvester/Wheatsheaf.

Porter, M. (1990). *The comparative advantages of nations*. London: Macmillan.

Prud'homme, R. (1995). The danger and decentralization. *The World Bank Research Observer, 10*(2), 201–206.

Rokkan, S., & Urwin, D. W. (1983). *Economy, territory, identity: Politics of West European peripheries*. London: Sage.

Rosenau, J. N. (1997). *Along the domestic-foreign Frontier: Exploring governance in a turbulent world*. Cambridge: Cambridge University Press.

Sbragia, A. M. (1992). Thinking about the European future: The uses of comparison. In A. M. Sbragia (Ed.), *Euro-politics: Institutions and policymaking in the "New" European community*. Washington, DC: Brookings Institution.

Scharpf, F. (1999). *Governing in Europe: Effective and democratic*. Oxford: Oxford University Press.

Schmitter, P. C. (1996). Imagining the future of the euro-polity with the help of new concepts. In G. Marks et al. (Eds.), *Governance in the European Union*. London: Sage.

Storper, M. (1997). *The regional world. Territorial development in a global economy*. New York: Guilford.

Veggeland, N. (2003). *Det nye demokratiet: et politisk laboratorium for partnerskap* [The new democracy: A political laboratory for partnership]. Kristiansand: Norwegian Academic Press.

Veggeland, N. (2009). *Taming the regulatory state: Politics and ethics*. Cheltenham, UK and Northampton, MA, Edward Elgar Publishing.

Veggeland, N. (Ed.). (2010a). *Innovative regulatory approaches. Coping with Scandinavian and European Union Politics*. New York: Nova Science Publishers.

Veggeland, N. (2010b). *Den nye reguleringsstaten. Idébrytninger og styringskonflikter*. Oslo: Gyldendal akademiske forlag.

Veggeland, N. (Ed.). (2016). *The current Nordic welfare state model*. New York: Nova Science Publishers.

Veggeland, N. (Ed.). (2017). *Administrative strategies of our time*. New York: Nova Science Publishers.

Wallace, H., Wallace, W., & Pollack, M. A. (2005). *Policy-making in the European Union*. Oxford: Oxford University Press.

Wallace, W. (1998). Government without statehood. In D. Wallace & H. Wallace (Eds.), *Policymaking in the European Union*. Oxford: Oxford University Press.

Weber, M. (2000). *Makt og byråkrati*. Oslo: Gyldendal.

Weiler, J. H. (1999). *The constitution of Europe*. Cambridge: Cambridge University Press.

Chapter 6
Translation of European Social Models

Social Models and Traditions[1]

The different administrative models and traditions of the European and Scandinavian countries are, by and large, characterized by social economies. This is demonstrated by their strong emphasis on balancing pure economic achievements with other goals, such as welfare, employment, social cohesion, leisure, and environmental sustainability. This implies that Europe is characterized by a larger public sector than other parts of the world (OECD Statistics 2005).

It is equally true that there are many European social sub-models. How many depends on the level of analysis, from the local to the national and to international levels. A coherent picture can, in other words, only be drawn if the analysis takes place at a reasonably high level of territorial aggregation (Knill 2001). The aim of this chapter is to group countries into appropriate sub-models in such a way that usefully explains how paths and administrative traditions perform innovation in the regulatory regimes (Majone 2003; Veggeland 1999).

We, by going beyond the macro-level of the European economic and social model, can distinguish the three sub-models of the Nordic Scandinavian, Anglo-Saxon, and Continental type (Knill 2001; EPC 2005). A Mediterranean and a new Eastern Europe model could also very well be recognized. A group of countries which have recently emerged from more than 50 years of Communist governance will, of course, have some common characteristics. It is, however, very likely that these countries will soon adopt one of the European models. This process is, indeed, probably already under way. The Southern model may be identifiable, but is not so useful in this analysis. Most of its characteristics can be found in (and probably come

---

[1]Per definition, social models embrace unnumbered regimes. My approach here is to elaborate transnational models containing international regimes. Fruitfully, S. Krasner (1983: 1) defines international regimes as "principles, norms, rules, and decision-making procedures around which actors expectations converge in a given issue-arena."

© Springer Nature Switzerland AG 2020
N. Veggeland, *Democratic Governance in Scandinavia*,
https://doi.org/10.1007/978-3-030-18270-0_6

from) the Continental model. Even the traditional historical West Nordic model (Norway, Iceland, and Denmark) contains characteristics that differ from the historical East Nordic tradition (Sweden and Finland), despite belonging to the common Scandinavian welfare state model. For example, the administrative tradition in the West Nordic tradition is that all public bureaucracy is, in principle, directly responsible to and controlled by the government, while in the East Nordic tradition, bureaucracy is partly exercised by an independent government agency, each controlled by an appointed board of experts. The characteristics of this have been identified and distinguished, and interesting conclusions have been analytically proposed (Gidlund and Jerneck 2000).

It is, for example, suggested that the East Nordic Scandinavian model, with its democratic expert management tradition based on a large number of self-ruling and fairly independent expert bodies, at arm's-length from the government working bureaucracy, is most open to adopting the regulatory state order. It is further suggested that the model has inspired basic NPM reforms[2] and distributed governance in the two-level setting found in the Anglo-American tradition, which has expanded increasingly since the 1970s (Pedersen 2006). On the other hand, the East Nordic Scandinavian model also easily later adopted reforms inspired by the Anglo-Saxon neoliberalism of the 1980s (OECD 2002). Ten years later, in the 1990s, the reform was adopted by the West Nordic states of Norway and Denmark (Gidlund 2000).

Comparison

There are, returning to the Anglo-Saxon, Nordic Scandinavian, and Continental models, some important differences and similarities between these models.

Firstly, the Anglo-Saxon and the Nordic models have become quite similar when it comes to the nature of relations between governments and markets. For example, the use of market-type mechanisms to provide government services (OECD 2005: 133). They are, however, very different when it comes to the size of government and state-centered planning and distributive social policies.

Secondly, the Nordic Scandinavian and the Continental models are more alike in terms of the public sector size, job security policies, and trade union relations. They are, however, very different in terms of government, labor market relations, and employment regulations (EPC 2005).

The Nordic Scandinavian model therefore emerges as a blend of the two large European models, the Anglo-Saxon model's emphasis on economic liberalism and the Continental model's emphasis on a large public sector and close relations to the labor market organizations (Jorgensen Overgaard and Vagnby 2005).

---

[2]For example, the "Next Steps Agencies" and "non-departmental bodies" in the UK; see OECD report 2002: 11.

Table 6.1 European models and tradition indicators

	Anglo-Saxon[a]	Nordic	Continental[b]
Government outlays as percent of nominal GDP	43–45%	48–58%	47–54%
Taxes as % of GDP (2003)	31–37%	45–51%	42–46%
Product market regulation (2003)	0.8–0.85	1.0–1.4	1.5–1.6
Unemployment rates (2004)	4.4–4.7	5.4–8.8	9.5–9.7

OECD statistics
[a]Represented by Ireland and the UK
[b]Represented by France and Germany

These positions can be demonstrated in a number of ways. One way is to look at the size of the public sector measured in terms of general government total outlays as a percent of nominal GDP and as total taxes as a percentage of GDP; see Table 6.1 below. This indicates the degree to which governments and country populations are willing to spend money on collective rather than individual issues in society. Welfare and social security issues are part of the collective approach. Table 6.1 shows that this willingness is lowest in the Anglo-Saxon tradition, and highest in the Nordic tradition, the Continental tradition being a close runner-up. This is perhaps not so strange considering that the historical roots and framework of the Scandinavian welfare state model are in the Prussian collective thinking of the late nineteenth century and Weberian neutral bureaucracy.

Attitudes to markets can also be measured in different ways. The OECD carried out a study in early 2005 to analyze a number of relevant issues, including an index of product market regulation. The three main models and traditions measured using this index give the results shown in Table 6.1, the Nordic tradition appearing to be a mixture model of the other two.

The product market regulation indexes in Table 6.1 indicate that the Anglo-Saxon administrative tradition and policy targets domestic deregulation of the product market and the simplification of rules in the framework of the EU regulatory regime. Domestic reregulation for correcting the market is more common and increasing for the Continental tradition. The Nordic model is shown to be a mixture of the two other models and traditions. This model has, since the 1980s, been transformed in the direction of greater market liberalism in some sectors. The state-centered path of the model, however, still tends to perform reregulations to correct the market and for collective and redistributive purposes. Regulatory performance has to be achieved innovatively in the framework of the EU/EEA regime, as it also does for the two other models and traditions (Veggeland 2006). Politically, the Nordic model continues to be based on a con-social order, i.e., bottom-up driven politics.

Anglo-Saxon Flexible Labor Market

When comparing the unemployment rate figures in Table 6.1, it is important to underline that labor market flexibility is defined and achieved in very different ways in the models. The Nordic Scandinavian and the Continental definitions must be distinguished from the Anglo-Saxon definition.

A flexible labor market could, in principle, mean that employers and workers agree to vary working conditions and working hours to meet the needs of business and the social and personal needs of the workers. However, in the Anglo-Saxon tradition, this usually means flexibility for employers, job insecurity, individualized wage payment, and low-paid wages and other poor working conditions for large groups of employees. Workers have low work security protection and are dismissed for profit and other reasons.

The definition of flexibility, in this tradition, stresses elements such as the possibility of wage differentiation based on performance-related pay and task measurement, part-time workplaces, contract-based appointments, job insecurity, no tariffs, low-paid social groups, health assurance linked to employers, and a passive Labor Market Policy. What came out of this was growing employment since the 1980s and low official unemployment rates as indicated in Table 6.1. However, inequality also increased (Pierson 2001a, b). People in work, however, often cling to the workplace they have despite bad working conditions, because their security is linked to the employer (Iversen 2005).

In short, labor market flexibility in the Anglo-Saxon framework is linked to job insecurity, poor work conditions, and high employment but low mobility. The EU regulatory state provokes Great Britain, the EU referendum causing withdrawal from the European Union, the so-called Brexit.

Continental Flexibility

The Continental and Nordic Scandinavian definition of labor market flexibility weights elements differently. These two traditions do, of course, deviate in certain ways, for example, trade unions having a stronger position in the traditional Continental model than in the Scandinavian, and more formal and rigid rules on the procedures of appointments and working conditions in the Continental model. Universal welfare and social security arrangements are a special characteristic of the Nordic Scandinavian model (Arter 1999; Einhorn and Logue 2003).

In both these models and traditions and their definition of labor market flexibility we find, as in the Anglo-Saxon model and since the 1980s, elements of wage differentiation by linking wages to the result of work task measurements and low-paid part-time work. In contrast, tariffs and equal access to health and social assurance, job security, and other work conditions are instead stressed in their definition. This makes them comparable, and according to Table 6.1, the Nordic

Scandinavian model is doing better than the Continental model with respect to the achievement of good employment.

However, which elements are important and which elements lead to the Nordic model being an alternative "in the middle" with regard to governance form is shown in Table 6.1 on employment policy?[3]

Maintaining employment in high-wage areas such as Western Europe requires flexibility of the workforce. This flexibility is in terms of previously acquired skills, a willingness to upgrade these skills constantly, and a readiness to leave jobs while upgrading skills (Iversen 2005). This could be seen as personal risk-taking but is, in reality, a strategy for job security.

Interestingly, the Continental model with its strong intervention on behalf of the employee unions through laws and procedures does not seem to provide security of this kind. It does provide compensation for the unemployed. But it does not, however, provide sufficient jobs. A persistent unemployment rate of more than 10% in Continental European countries demonstrates that this model has serious imbalances, runs a very strong risk of financing problems in the longer term, and thereby loses legitimacy in the EU struggle to develop a promising social model for Europe and an enlarged EU.

Nordic Scandinavian Flexicurity

One important feature of the in-between Scandinavian labor market situation, indicated in Table 6.1, is the flexibility of the Active Labor Market Policy and the employee unions combined with social security policy for the unemployed, i.e., what is called "flexicurity"[4] policy, a term discussed earlier in our book (EPC 2005). This policy helps explain why the Scandinavian welfare state model may, in this respect, be sustainable despite the high costs paid by taxpayers. The key to its success is that the employment service has been turned from providing passive compensation for unemployment to providing services which help the unemployed develop their skills and actively search for jobs. This is probably a much better use of public money than paying 10% or more of the population for not working, which is a bad solution for economic and welfare state sustainability (OECD 2005).

Contemporary Nordic countries are achieving a better result through employing its workforce in a flexible way. This is most likely due to three elements:

- The universal health and social assurance arrangements
- The active Labor Market Policy
- The transformation of earlier rigorous regulation of its labor markets to softer regulations of an innovative and satisfactory character

---

[3]I owe great debt to the analyses of the EPC 2005 working paper in the following.
[4]Labor market flexibility combined with social security.

It is, in contrast, very difficult in Continental Europe to change the workforce, to alter the make-up of skills, and thereby to offer flexibility to employers and job security. This is, however, quite easy in the Scandinavian model. Adaptation to a fast-changing labor market through lifelong learning is, in general, accepted in the Scandinavian model. A further social driving force behind flexibility in the Nordic Scandinavian model and in the framework of mobility is that changing job or employer or being out of work because of upgrading personal skills does not mean the loss of health and social security rights. These rights are universal and do not depend on employment or employer (Iversen 2005). This phenomenon is of greatest importance in sustainable local and regional development in the framework of the new regionalism and competing regions (Veggeland 2000).

The modernized contemporary Nordic Scandinavian model represents, in this context, an administrative innovation in a European setting. The innovation is linked to the creation of necessary flexibility in a fast-changing and globalized labor market, but within a framework of universal social security. We shall see that the innovation of flexicurity policy, as an appropriate solution that is based on positive feedback, has not come up by an accident but as part of a path-dependent development linked to the tradition of the Scandinavian welfare state model in general (Arter 1999).

Promoting Flexibility and Innovation

Innovation reforms as repercussions of social model paths, such as the Nordic Scandinavian flexicurity, claim to empower citizens and increase legitimacy. However, in the real world, public authorities usually find themselves facing trade-offs[5] or even outright contradictions. The possible contradiction between two or more appealing propositions is not necessarily, but can be, obvious. If we construct society as a quadrant of appealing social models and their concerns, in terms of the European models, then four feasible trade-offs arise.

In our framework, there is a contradiction between a regulatory state-centered and a regulatory market-centered model. Inevitably, empowerment of the state diminishes the ability of the market to rule and set the agenda. There is a trade-off.

On the other hand, a state-centered social model seems, in Fig. 6.1, to encompass well a dominant family concern in terms of offering social security and welfare for all. A market-centered social model similarly will normally appreciate civil society actors, the NGOs, and their activities as arm's-length independent actors from the government, the encouragement of NGOs in this tradition being viewed as being partners against state bureaucracy and conformism.

---

[5]Trade-offs define where more of one desideratum, or lessening one problem, inevitably diminishes some other wished-for quality or increases a different problem.

Fig. 6.1 The quadrant of
trade-offs and social model
concerns

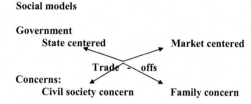

Decision-makers are obliged to balance between the things they want. More of all cannot, however, feasibly be achieved at the same time. Indeed, more of one entails having less of another. In our framework, the thesis is that the policy direction decision-makers chose to place the point of balance so that more of one thing and less of another depends on the paths derived from basic social models and administrative traditions. Trade-offs challenge the legitimacy of the decisions made, which encourages policy makers to initiate research programs and innovative processes. Scholarly advice, in the framework of rational choice, tends to make the conditions and the impacts of the options as transparent and sustainable as possible and is often vital for the purpose of legitimacy.

Trade-offs are between regulatory state centralism and civil society concern. This is inevitable, as top-down management normally does not encourage bottom-up movements. On the contrary, it often bars such movements and thereby con-social interaction, i.e., the political consensus approach is not given priority over family concerns (Weiler 1999). The thesis is that this type of trade-off is found as a path-dependent policy dilemma, coming out of the Continental social model and its regimes.

Trade-offs also occur between regulatory market centralism and family concerns, because universal social security arrangements do not exist for the employees of a family nor for the family. Employers are responsible for employees while they work for them but, in a socioeconomic sense, not for the wealth of the families. The family is not given priority over NGOs as part of the basic social capital and condition for a sustainable economy. The thesis here is that this trade-off type is most likely to be found as a path-dependent policy dilemma coming out of the Anglo-Saxon market-focused social model and its regimes.

Table 6.1 points out repercussions of the state-centered Nordic model policies, decision-making results coming out of a blending, an in-between, of the other two. This most likely is also true for our quadrant approach and the trade-offs. Hence, the thesis is that the trade-offs of the Nordic model, as a model of balancing policy, frame a policy of giving priority to both civil society and family concerns. Even so, Nordic decision-makers cannot feasibly have more of all at the same time.

The Nordic Scandinavian thesis therefore needs a supplement. Neither NGOs nor families hardly recognize a downward-bound priority related to trade-offs. However, since the 1980s and the Nordic model internationally being directly confronted by the Anglo-Saxon model's policies due to an increasingly open economy, likely trade-offs have made the Nordic countries more market centered compared to that expected from the tradition of being prototypes of state-centered regimes. We know

Table 6.2 Outsourcing of public services

Public purchase of goods and services vs. in-house provision. Selected countries

Country		Rank	
UK	···	(1)	
US	···	(2)	> 50 %
Norway	···	(3)	
Switzerland	······································	(4)	
Sweden	···································	(5)	
New Zealand	································	(6)	
Australia	·······························	(7)	
Finland	····························	(8)	
Netherlands	···························	(9)	
Iceland	··························	(10)	
Germany	························	(11)	
Canada	·····················	(12)	
Denmark	····················	(13)	< 50 %
Austria	·················	(14)	
Luxembourg	···············	(15)	
Belgium	·············	(16)	
Ireland	············	(17)	
Spain	············	(18)	
France	··········	(19)	
Italy	··········	(20)	
Portugal	··········	(21)	

```
0   10   20   30   40   50   60   70   80   90 %
```

Source: OECD (2005): Modernizing Government

little about what social repercussions followed as outputs of the transformation of their inherent regimes, and which transformations if any should be noted as innovations. One example of a repercussion should be looked upon as a regulatory innovation and as having a positive impact on regional development.

Regional Impact

OECD ranking is given below of the impetus for outsourcing public services of selected countries.

Table 6.2 features interesting aspects of the modernization of the public service sector, with respect to our context. The OECD data figures (2005) envisage the market-type mechanism of outsourcing as being heavily in use in Europe. It is, however, significantly more widespread in the English-speaking Anglo-Saxon countries and the Scandinavian countries than in the Continental European states. Are there grounds for asking why this is so?

As expected, the percentages put the two main states of the market-oriented Anglo-Saxon administrative tradition at the top of the outsourcing ranking. In the EU member state of the UK, only 22% of government services are in-house, 78% being the outcome of outsourcing. In the USA, the respective figures are 35 and 65%, in New Zealand 45 and 55%, and in Australia 50 and 50%. Switzerland, being outside the Anglo-Saxon tradition, and with less than 50%, in-house might be due to the relatively small public sector.

The positions of the Nordic states in the graph might, perhaps, be unexpected in terms of these belonging to the state-centered Scandinavian administrative tradition.

Norway is ranked as the third greatest user of the market-type mechanism of outsourcing in public procurement of services, 40% in-house provision of public services and 60% from outsourcing. Sweden is fifth, following just behind with around 45 and 55%. Finland is eighth, Iceland tenth, and Denmark fourteenth, all comprehensively using outsourcing (40–50%) as a mechanism for providing public services.

The Nordic Scandinavian figures must be said to be strongly aberrant when compared with the two main EU member states belonging to the Continental administrative tradition. In the Continental tradition and in line with that expected, the market-type mechanism of outsourcing in the public sector has been, according to the graph, used only modestly. The biased path-dependent policy of Germany generated 60% in-house provision and 40% from outsourcing and correspondingly France 75 and 25%. The latter figures reveal a very traditional and strong state-centered provision of services, one for which it is questioned whether it is dynamic and flexible enough?

Microeconomic Effects

The related aberrant Nordic figures for the rate of outsourcing versus in-house provision of public services should not be explained as an empirical turnout that is biased by the path dependence of the administrative tradition. Instead, the high rate of outsourcing seems to be related to another path, the path of a Nordic tradition carrying certain institutional values, namely the value of "small is beautiful." Let us test this hypothesis.

Three alternatives exist:

(a) There was an adaptation to the EU directive, and a surprisingly extensive use of the market and competition in relation to that required by the administrative tradition.

(b) An adaptation occurred, influenced by new liberalistic Anglo-Saxon ideology and by the New Public Management (NPM) principle, as can be easily interpreted from Table 6.2.
(c) Public administration in the two Scandinavian countries were reregulated to achieve political objectives and therefore performed innovatively, because they broke away from their traditional path dependence.

Let us examine this more closely. One EU adopted regulation from the early 1990s on public procurement demands was that all public purchases of non-in-house provisions of goods and services over the marginal cost level of Euro 200,000 are obliged to be exposed to market competition through tendering and outsourcing. This takes place through open or partly open tendering and bidding rounds, the provisions being contracted out to the private providers that win each of the many bidding rounds.

This is the brief background. We are focusing on the EEA negotiations at the beginning of 1990 between EFTA countries and the EU agreement for access to the EU's inner market. The EEA agreement was entered into. Sweden and Finland, previously EFTA countries, instead of entering this agreement, in 1994 became EU members. Norway and Iceland continued as EEA countries. The EEA agreement included the EU's national set of rules and directives regarding public purchasing of products and services. Procedures and an upper limit of Euro 200,000 were established for such purchases at that time. Purchases for lower values did not require competition and bidding administration. Purchases over this value were included in the directive, and thereby placed under surveillance by the EU and, for Norway and Iceland, the ESA EFTA agency.

As in many other EU member states, there were at the time major obstacles and skeptical attitudes to the introduction of outsourcing in Scandinavian societies. This was due to a popular and social-democratic concern about private sector involvement in traditional public activities. The other concern related to very few services not being outsourced, despite great variety technically. The lack of clarity on the issue of which "services of general interest"[6] ought to remain in-house provisions and which should be exposed to commercial competition was defined as an attack on the universal welfare state. The challenge to existing public service provision also triggered resistance from affected public employees, unions, and their political allies. Lastly, the outsourcing game was perceived as a game in which private big businesses would come out as winners and thereby threaten the Scandinavian "small is beautiful" concept, i.e., small and medium-sized businesses (SMBs) and local and regional economies.

At that time, and in the wake of the general skeptical attitudes to the market-type mechanism of outsourcing, the Scandinavian states introduced a reregulation, which

---

[6]The term "services of general interest" is by the EU defined as public services, which the government provides and should provide under universal obligation. The diversification of this type of services for in-house provision or outsourcing is still heavily disputed in the Union; see the dispute on the "service directive."

was influenced by the EEA agreement and probably by the "small is beautiful" tradition. Norway and Sweden set the upper limit for bidding much lower than the EU regime required: NOK 200,000 for Norway and SEK 200,000 for Sweden. Scandinavian bidding limits have now increased to more than a million krone in these countries. The decision resulted in a much more extensive use of bidding administration and outsourcing than the EU's marginal value for public purchasing would have given. This partly explains their high ranking in Table 6.1. The decision was legal because the EU directive contained no decisions against lower national limits for biddings and competition. The directive could therefore be interpreted freely. This represents an extreme, as most public purchases of provisions would exceed the marginal level, due to Scandinavian high price levels.

What came out of this independent and innovative change in outsourcing and the Scandinavian regulatory solution in the wake of this specific Europeanization mode of institutional penetration?

On the positive side, there was an incitement to small and middle-sized private providers (SMBs) to adjust to the markets created by the outsourcing form of public administration. Small providers/businesses with low investment ability gained the opportunity to participate and adjust to public procurement and tendering because of the "beautiful" low regulatory cost level. SMBs, taking advantage of being small, numerous, and flexible, came out as winners in the vast number of bidding rounds. As contractors, they contributed to the creation of important employment and services locally all over the Scandinavian countries and thereby to regional development.

I have presented just one case of trade-offs. Similar cases, of course, exist. We, however, know very little about them and how they came into being under regulatory state schemes and in the wake of trade-offs. We therefore need more multidisciplinary comparative research to get answers.

References

Arter, D. (1999). *Scandinavian politics today.* Manchester: Manchester University Press.
Einhorn, E. S., & Logue, J. (2003). *Modern welfare states. Scandinavian politics and policy in the global age.* Westport, CT: Praeger.
EPC Working Paper. (2005). *The Nordic model: A recipe for European success?* (EPC Working Paper No. 20).
Gidlund, J. (2000). *Nordic bifurcation in post-wall Europe.* Op. cit. Gidlund, J. and Jerneck, M. (eds.) (2000: 231–263).
Gidlund, J., & Jerneck, M. (Eds.). (2000). *Local and regional governance in Europe. Evidence from Nordic regions.* Cheltenham: Edward Elgar.
Iversen, T. (2005). *Capitalism. Democracy and welfare.* Cambridge: Cambridge University Press.
Jorgensen Overgaard, L., & Vagnby, B. (2005). *What happens to spatial and physical planning in Denmark after the local government reform?* Paper submitted to RGA's RSA International Conference, University of Aalborg.
Knill, C. (2001). *The Europeanization of the national administrations.* Cambridge: Cambridge University Press.

Krasner, S. (1983). Structural causes and regime consequences, regimes as intervening variables. In S. Krasner (Ed.), *International regimes*. London: Cornell University Press.

Majone, G. (2003). *The politics of regulation and European regulatory institutions*. Op. cit. Hayward, J. and Menon, A. (eds.) (2003: 297–312).

OECD. (2002). *Distributed public governance. Agencies, authorities and other government bodies*. Paris: OECD Publishing.

OECD. (2005). *Modernising government. The way forward*. Paris: OECD Publishing.

OECD Statistics (2005): *OECD economic outlook* (Vol. 1, no 77). Paris: OECD Publishing.

Pedersen, T. H. (2006). *Tonivåmodellen – et barn av den nordiske modellen eller forveksling på fødestuen*. Paper presented, Kongsvinger Sept. 2006. Lillehammer: Centre for Public Policy Innovation (CPPI).

Pierson, P. (2001a). *Post-industrial pressures on the mature welfare states*. Op. cit. Pierson, P. (ed.) (2001: 80–106).

Pierson, P. (Ed.). (2001b). *The new politics of the welfare state*. Oxford: Oxford University Press.

Veggeland, N. (1999). *The arrival of the regulatory state. Global challenge and state response*. (Paper). Lillehammer: Lillehammer University College.

Veggeland, N. (2000). *Den ny regionalismen. Flernivåstyring og europeisk integrasjon*. Bergen: Fagbokforlaget.

Veggeland, N. (2006). *Public sector innovation in regulatory regimes. On Scandinavian path-dependence*. Paper presented at Colombia University, New York. Lillehammer: Lillehammer University College, Center for Public Policy Innovation.

Weiler, J. H. (1999). *The Constitution of Europe*. Cambridge: Cambridge University Press.

Chapter 7
Administrative Traditions: And the "Trilemma"

Introduction

The purpose of this chapter is to show that the administration of a modern regulatory welfare state is complex. The state meets the challenge of the "trilemma" outlined as exclusion of objectives. Social policy formation fundamentally relies on the outcome of the debate on the future of the European welfare state. Social policy formation is, from the perspective of the political-economic approach, a dependent variable in both European integration policy and national administrative traditions. However, the national state does not act in a sovereign manner in relation to the European Union (EU) nor in relation to domestic member actors. All are confronted with the so-called trilemma aspect, a term first introduced by the US social scientist Torben Iversen (2005). In this chapter, we follow up his analysis and show the difficult choices that confront policy-makers at the different administrative levels due to this trilemma and its trade-offs. New Public Management ideas are dominant and for the time being confront the ruling administrative social traditions of Western Europe. In this chapter, I conclude that a European agreement on a social choice, related to overcoming the trilemma, must be accomplished to save the welfare state model as we know it. The traditional Nordic welfare state model provides an example.

Parts of this chapter have been previously published under open access as Veggeland, N. (2018). Administrative Traditions—and the Problem of the "Trilemma." Studies in Asian Social Science, Vol. 5 (1). Sciedu Press.

"Spillover" Processes

The study of international policy in traditional political science in the years following World War II tended to use theories that explain integration in relation to the development of institutions and the regulation of the relationships through agreements between sovereign states (Rosamond 2000). The development of Western welfare states in the 1950s and 1960s and until the mid-1970s took place under highly favorable circumstances, aided by continuous growth in the economies, so allowing governments to manage national budgetary control (Veggeland 2016; Tinbergen 1965). Political economic analysis, therefore, characteristically emphasized a national, state-centered perspective that was bound both to the techno-economic paradigm rooted in Keynesian state intervention and principles of effective demand and to the socio-institutional paradigm of Weberian bureaucracy (Olsen 2005; Brunsson 2011).

This is particularly true of the realist school (Cini 2004a, b). Realism claims that international politics is about interaction of self-interested states in an anarchic environment, in which no supranational authority is capable of securing order and reducing risks. According to the theory "is centered on the view that nation states are the key actors in international affairs and the key political relations between states are channeled primarily via national governments." Thus, realists have focused exclusively on governmental institutions and actors and their taming roles in internationalization and transnational cooperation (Veggeland 2017).

The same is true for spokesmen of the intergovernmental approach. They point out that there is significant evidence of intergovernmental bargaining and consensus-building techniques as dominant modes of policy-making in many areas (Moravcsik 1993, 1998). They understand that, despite an anarchical environment, there is some potential for order on the basis of international cooperation. It is especially true when governments enter into negotiations and bargaining processes and reach legally binding agreements, so establishing order and favorable cooperative networks. The EU states are an example of such cooperation (Hoffmann 1996; Moravcsik 1998). This is the traditional community method of integration based on hard regulation. The method depends on bargaining processes and consensus building, with member state governments as actors. The output takes the form of laws and regulations, and ever more authority gravitates to the supranational regime of the EU, which also becomes an independent actor of defined political areas in continuing bargaining processes. Intergovernmentalism is not only of relevance to EU politics. It also refers to a type of decision-making and partnership building that occurs within all international network organizations.

These theories of realism and intergovernmental approach do, however, ignore central functional national actors such as financial agencies, regulatory arm's-length administrations and other governmental bodies, private businesses, and NGOs, acting in trans-border networks. Subnational political administrative actors are also ignored, including municipalities and regions (Anderson 1994). In the global age, these extra-governmental actors take advantage of their beneficiaries' networking abilities and through this transfer their demands, expectations, and their loyalties from central government to new centers (March and Olsen 2005; Veggeland 2013). Cross-border and transnational initiatives are taken, and agreements are settled out of the remit of the central government.

The neo-functionalism strand, another dominant school of understanding integration and the development of network organizations, consequently has extended the nongovernmental perspective and recognized that political goals can only be realized if strategic thinking includes "beyond-government" actors, that is, socio-economic sectors, interest groups, and acting individuals (Haas 1958; Nye 1971). Beyond governments, such actors cooperate in networks and develop themselves through the advancement of agreements and contracts, this not being rooted in trust but in mistrust.[1] The advancement both of functional and benefit-making network extensions and of pressure for further integration of other sectors and interest groups is termed "functional spillover" processes.

The occurrence of "spillover" processes and the concomitant increase of mutual dependence between increasing numbers of actors become predominant (Strøby Jensen 2004). The option actors have for exiting partnerships, moreover, exacerbates these conditions of vulnerability. These conditions reflect the vulnerability of the decision-making processes of the European Community, which is "spilling over" into the direction of an ever-closer Union. As elaborated by Ernst Haas and other scholars (Haas 1958), European integration commenced with an initial decision by six governments to place a certain sector, in this case coal and steel, under the authority of a common central authority, the institutions of the Coal and Steel Union. There was enormous pressure to extend the authority of these institutions into neighboring policy areas, which ended with the Treaty of Rome as a part of a first round. Neo-functionalists had therefore predicted the expansion and deepening of European integration, an increasing number of member states, and the involvement of many other issues, such as monetary policy and service industries. Despite legally binding treaties and regulations, the neo-functional school understood that organizational dynamics entails vulnerability, in the sense that the processes generate unforeseen consequences that may not be acceptable to member states and extragovernmental actors. In a taming perspective, the threat of the exit option may deliberately change the development path (Veggeland 2004).

Neo-functionalists think, from the perspective of economic-base theory and typically link politics and social-institutional paradigms as a "functional spillover" from economics, that is, techno-economic paradigms. Functional economies tend to adopt functional institutions, and dysfunctional economies tend to adopt dysfunctional institutions. Using this neo-functional conceptualization, we might identify the regulatory state order of institutions as being a "functional spillover" from monetarist and supply-side economics. If the international economic system of this

---

[1]Mistrust, in this context, means in the sense of a calculated risk option for withdrawal from the interest-based partnership cooperation.

kind becomes disordered, then the regulatory institutional system will, accordingly, be put under immediate pressure for change.

Joseph S. Nye (1971) therefore defines functional "spillover" as a way of reestablishing the balance after an imbalance has arisen between political organization and the functional power connected with economic market forces. Functional "spillover" takes place when inadequate state organization undermines the effectiveness of politics and planning in the different social sectors, as the Keynesian state did in the 1970s. We may consider what is termed deregulation and re-regulation as consequences of functional "spillover" from market-making and market-correcting policies.

Political "spillover" occurs when national, subnational, and supranational arm's-length bodies, interest groups, and other bodies create additional pressure for the further extension of mutual networks of cooperation. If these demands are not fulfilled, then cooperation dissolves. The latter outcome is an indication of partnership vulnerability, rooted either in rational choices or in mistrust and conflict. Another outcome might realistically be the establishment of new regulatory bodies in order to provide necessary services to control the rules of the game of cooperation or to correct the market through re-regulation. However, this latter solution should make governments and other stakeholders at all levels of decision-making think critically about the necessity of taking into consideration the already existing numerous arm's-length bodies (OECD 2002; Veggeland 2004). We have already encountered this phenomenon in the different forms of institutional modes of the regulatory state.

The neo-functionalists have a pluralistic but somewhat deterministic view on network development and on the attempts that participating actors make to regulate corporations, bargaining processes, and agreement settlements. What is underemphasized is the vulnerability of those "spillover" processes, probably because of the neo-functionalist tendency to regard "spillover" processes deterministically. What is missing, however, is the intergovernmentalist view that recognizes that governments undertake certain activities that may cause friction or totally undermine further network developments and expansions (Pollack 2005). Neo-functionalists are, furthermore, also guilty of neglecting the "spillover" of regional and local political structures. In contrast, the liberal strand of intergovernmental approach, which includes a liberal theory of national bottom-up preference formation, recognizes this phenomenon (Moravcsik 1998).

In our analysis above, we have tried to show how the state apparatus together with numerous other actors participate in national and transnational network arenas, so creating agreement-based structures of regulatory governance as part of the regulatory state order (Veggeland 2017). Public–public and public–private partnerships also operate in these arenas. They progress, but at the cost of generating vulnerability. This susceptibility partly reflects the increasing "hollowing out" of traditional sovereignty of the European national state. At a high political level, the pooling of national sovereignty in the EU is, however, essential. Equally important is the parallel movement at the national level, namely the pooling of state authority in partnerships and arm's-length governmental bodies and agencies.

The neo-functionalists have noted the essential point in a pluralistic perspective that new industrial forms of organization and arenas for regulation have created functional and political "spillover" effects as a consequence of the building of new economies. The new forms in the industrial sector reflect, in some sense, the function of fragmentations in the public sector. There has been a change in the market forms of production; the character of production has changed from Fordism to post-Fordism (Amin 1994). Fordism was intimately bound to the Keynesian economy and the need for balance between an interventionist state and the business sector. Compacted, hierarchical organized businesses of mass production confronted a monopoly-based hierarchical state, in a policy framework of scale. At the time, the form represented a stable mode of macroeconomic growth.

The transformation of this market form of production to Schumpeter-inspired post-Fordism occurred in the 1970s. The compact fordism hierarchy structure was split into small, flexible, consumer-adapted business units. It is commonly accepted that three theoretical approaches, each offering a somewhat different perspective, together capture the essential characteristics of this post-Fordist political economy (Amin 1994). These are:

1. The regulation approach understands the transformation to post-Fordism as a somewhat parallel process of industrial fragmentation to the establishment of arm's-length bodies and agencies in the public sector. The reconstruction of the mother company into smaller branch firms inhere a belief in the principle of "steering without rowing," in the economic interest of more effective indirect management by means of the distant regulation of subsidiaries.
2. The flexible specialization and customer-adapted approach understands this transformation as a fix for the demand for fast changes in production, technology, and internal organization to satisfy customers. All of these aim at making the business more productive and competitive.
3. The neo-Schumpeterian approach understands the transformation as an adjustment of the "socio-institutional paradigm" in the business sector to the new "techno-economic paradigm" of the regulatory state. Aside from competition in the market, a diversity of smaller units delivering items and services to the mother company could encourage "creative destruction" and industrial innovation.
4. Creative destruction and innovation in the business sector indicates risky but beneficial undertakings and dynamics in growing economies. The vulnerability attached to economic recessions appears in the sense of threatening overall destruction.
5. Smaller units delivering items and services to the mother company have their basis in the principle of "just-in-time" delivery in order to be effective organizations. Such a principle is, by definition, vulnerable. For example, a strike at one firm or an infrastructure failure at another will, for a period of time, disrupt the whole production cycle of the company. A strike at one unit will negatively affect other workers' conditions elsewhere in the production chain, which raises ethical considerations.

6. Vulnerability of this kind creates a need for wide-reaching regulations and measurements of goal achievement. Post-Fordism, therefore, biases the building of the regulatory state.

Dependence, Vulnerability, and Sensitivity

We may take, as a starting point, those neo-functionalist network theories that do not allocate to the state a central position, as is the case with realists. Several scholars have elaborated the social-institutional paradigm of the weakened national state with respect to dependence and interdependence effects caused by network mechanisms. As early as 1971, Joseph S. Nye published the article "Comparing Common Markets: A Revised Neo-Functional Model." Later, Nye with Robert O. Keohane published *Power and Interdependence: World Politics in Transition* (1977). Their theories are well-suited to throwing new and better light upon the development of forms of interaction in networks, which have occupied a dominant position in the 1980s and 1990s. They assert that the state does not act in a sovereign manner in relation to international and domestic actors in the market, nor in relation to political and administrative actors that have clearly acquired a position of relative autonomy within the state system. Two important concepts in this respect are "interdependence" and "network integration" with regard to partnership formations such as the EU (Veggeland 2004).

Dependence means that one actor unilaterally becomes influenced by the actions of other actors. *Interdependence* refers to a situation of mutual dependence, as is the case in national and international arenas of network governance. Interdependence does not presume likeness between parties. Partnership formations based on bargaining instead mean that power connected to political and knowledge-based resources favors one of the parties. The concept of interdependence normally only becomes defined descriptively, without an evaluation of its desirability having been made. Interdependence may, however, result in economic and social inequality, what EU language calls a "lack of economic and social cohesion" between states, regions, and social groups (Keating and Loughlin 1997). This also applies to the issue of social-institutional standards.

With reference to interdependence, Keohane and Nye (1977) proposed *sensitivity* and *vulnerability* as two dimensions of interaction, both of which need to be tamed. Nye has later elaborated this notion further and has suggested a "three-dimensional chess model" as a basic term of reference to high politics (2004). In the first dimension, strategic military concepts of power are developed, and in the middle, second dimension, techno-economic concepts define the competitive strength of the state. Lastly, in the third dimension, supranational networks of World Wide Web transactions expand the transmission of things such as money transfers, information, and messages. There are also computer hackers and terrorist groups and the presence of corruption, unethical investments, and pandemic and environmental threats.

States operate more or less successfully in all three arenas of this chess model. Nevertheless, a high degree of vulnerability and sensitivity dominates the game.

As a case in point, Nye critically puts the contemporary USA into this game and carries out an evaluation according to the framework of the three-dimensional chess model. The USA dominates the military play dimension as a superpower of the world. In the second area of play, other economic players such as Europe or the EU, China, Japan, and Russia compete well and put pressure on the US economy. The contemporary US loan-driven economy furthermore makes this play dimension vulnerable, for reasons embedded in its own monetary system (a statement supported by F. Lordon 2008). However, as a player in the bottom arena, the USA is really in trouble and has turned out to become especially vulnerable. We need only mention the presence of international terrorist networks in this arena.

According to Nye, the USA has not been playing this game well. It has first and foremost played internationally and has tried to tame the top arena, that is, the dimension of military strength and forces. This had to turn out as a strategy of failure. Military power serves the chess player poorly in winning games related to the two other dimensions of the model, particularly the lowest dimension. Dependence, interdependence, and "spillover" effects in the unbalanced chess games that the contemporary USA has been playing for years increase its vulnerability. President Donald Trump continues to play these games.

According to Nye, environmental problems belong to the dimension of the worldwide arena and respect no order. They pay no attention to national and administrative boundaries. They are human-made, but the disorder they create is connected to vulnerable natural ecosystems of interdependent elements. Ecosystems are complex and have their own boundaries, ranging from the local to the global scale. This is the physical side of environmental problems, but there is also a regulatory side. The problems have arisen partly as a result of many national and local political decisions and interventions being implemented without any overall planning and coordination and also partly as a consequence of the many decisions taken by actors competing in the market, the middle dimension of the chess model. The environmental problems, which are created by both private and public activity, therefore appear as a mixed-dimensional problem.

Dependence on natural goods and resources in relation to human existence and economy leads to regulatory interdependence between states, regions, organizations, and businesses. The effects of the ecosystem create vulnerability where regulatory authorities, whose efforts are indispensible for a multidimensional winning game, are lacking. Without a rational overview of networks and mechanisms, environmental problems will expand, so decreasing efficiency in the economic dimension, further disturbing the international balance (if there happens to be any) in the defense and security dimension.

Damage caused by slippages of environmental waste management often crosses boundaries, but can often be treated one dimensionally. Regulation and planning for sustainable development is not, however, an issue that only affects relationships between states. A pluralistic multidimensional perspective is necessary here, which involves not just integrated cooperation between governments and economic actors.

Political actions and ethical behavior are also required at all levels, from the global to the local. The EU principle of subsidiarity, that is, devolution of decision-making competence to the lowest possible level but high enough to be effective, formulated in the Maastricht Treaty of 1992, offers guidance to the multidimensional perspective. Consciousness of global environmental problems, along with processes of internationalization in general, increases awareness of the complex, interdependent bonds and structures that exist between an indefinite number of global, national, and local actors and thereby increases awareness of the sensitivity and vulnerability inherent in these connective formations.

As is commonly known, the complex economic enterprises of post-Fordism barely heed national and administrative boundaries in their market transactions (Amin 1994). A municipality, a region, and a state are *sensitive* to the types of interdependence created in the system of enterprises established on the basis of flexible specialization and new technology. But because of the high level of dependence, the post-Fordist system of production turns out to be *vulnerable*. Vulnerability concerns not only the economic dimension and its relationships but also the operations between states, regions, and private actors in the growing global market, acknowledged by the European cooperative network, the EU.

Vulnerability also relates to the challenge of social inequality when policies for sustainable economic zero growth come up. Poor people may suffer most, which impacts the ideals of the Scandinavian welfare state thinking. Regulatory state measures seem so far to mind the growing inequality coming up in all the Scandinavian national states.

Interdependence and vulnerability create a need for social policies and wide-reaching agreements and regulations. Regulatory measurement assumes coordinated political arenas of decision-making and implementation at all levels. The general framework of national and international laws, special laws, the use of management by objectives, benchmarking, and the evaluation and comparison of output are all important. This applies to the sustainable development of modern communication and transport, the exploitation of both sea and land resources, industrial spillage, and technological development. It narrows the "free room" which each state, region, municipality, and enterprise has when exercising their sovereignty.

Usually, pluralists do not operate with any clear distinction between domestic and foreign policy (Dahl-Eriksen 1997). On the contrary, the assertion is made that the division between inner and outer sovereignty is increasingly difficult to maintain in the light of processes of internationalization. This means, for planning and targeting sustainable development, that domestic planning must be integrated with international planning actions. Correspondingly, authorities with legitimate power can sanction those who break agreements. These sanctions must, however, be enforced at the different levels as an administrative consequence of political "spillover" effects.

A fundamental characteristic of the theories of interdependence is that they do not in principle regard the international system as a set of different national and regional economic and social systems. This view means giving up the belief in an anarchistic international system, in which cooperation and institutional development only involves questions of security. The cooperation and institutional development understanding of the processes of internationalization represents a natural development of the position advocated by realists and rationalists in political science. This asserts that it is not possible to break with the principle of state sovereignty and that no global authority is capable of taming conflicts of interest and securing order (Cini 2004a, b). Intervening in the domestic interests of a national state is forbidden by international law. Globalization and interdependence, in the sense of the networked society (Castells 1996), provides a foundation for changing these laws. New forms of regulation, based on the EU, can support this change without abandoning pluralistic and democratic forms of state. New modes of interacting, cross-border planning, and governance furthermore must be developed to match the new situation and the liabilities of sensitivity and vulnerability (Krasner 1983).

The Search for Security and Safety

Let us revisit the European models of administrative traditions. At least three general models have, through the history and different phases of European integration, formed the foundations for matching social-institutional paradigms with new structures to counteract repercussions of socio-institutional sensitivity, vulnerability, and risks. These are the Continental, Anglo-Saxon, and Nordic Scandinavian models and their different administrative traditions (Knill 2001; Veggeland 2007).

The Continental model naturally was dominant from the launching of the European integration process and from the adoption of the Treaty of Rome in the 1950s by the founder inner six Continental states, Germany, France, Italy, and the three Benelux countries. This administrative tradition created path dependence of state-focused con-federalism and interventionism as a reflection of the Keynesian state (Millward 2000). From the Continental tradition came the policy inspiration to embrace European social partners, the European umbrella trade union (ETUC), and the private and public employers' interest organizations, Unice (now Businesseurope) and CEEP, respectively, to the negotiation table (de Buck 2004). The goal was to tame and correct the integration process by putting social concerns on the agenda. A sort of Continental corporatist style was the result. The Maastricht Treaty from 1992 introduced the "social dimension" of the Community, with the expressed goal being to create arenas for deliberative talks and to thereby reach consensus instead of conflict on social and labor market issues. The Anglo-Saxon state of the United Kingdom is exempted from the EU social dimension. Now in the dilemma of Brexit, the United Kingdom still remains outside this facet of EU policy.

The dominance of the Continental tradition lasted until the end of the 1980s (Urwin 1996). The adoption of the Single European Act in 1987 and the introduction of the Single European Market process one year later marked a fundamental contextual change (Austvik 2002). The strategies of minimizing the state and marketizing the public sector, from the Anglo-Saxon origin, became dominant policies (Pollitt and Bouckaert 2004). The member states furthermore decided to deregulate, and re-regulate, to create a territorially wider, borderless, single European market. The new regulatory state order of the EU took over. We might say that this caused the transformation of the social-institutional paradigm, which is much in accordance with the Anglo-Saxon social model and market-orientated administrative tradition.

How did such a transformation occur? When the United Kingdom joined the European Community (EC) in 1972 as a major member state, global recession, inflation, unemployment, and stagflation had reached the shores of all member states. The crises biased and pressed forward the change, or at least the modification, of the techno-economic and socio-institutional paradigms. The Anglo-Saxon model and the tradition of organizing governance became dominant and turned the Community's method away from state-focused con-federalism and interventionism toward the regulatory state scheme, which is based on market-centered policies, modes of New Public Management, and supply-side economics. The concept of the social dimension and the involvement of social partners in negotiations, along with sensitive issues such as work conditions and social and labor market reforms, were temporarily taken off the record (Koukiadis 2006).

During the 1990s, both the ability failure of the EU to compete in the global economy and the democratic and legitimacy deficit became central issues, threatening the core identity of the Union. When the Soviet Union collapsed, the political situation in Europe also changed radically, the poor Eastern Europe states wanting membership status in the "rich men's club," and the Amsterdam Treaty of 1997 opening the door to them. Ten new states joined the Union in 2004, and two more in 2007, bringing with them heavy social and economic burdens that were expected and immediately felt. Reforms were necessary, and they were formulated, agreed on, and implemented as socio-institutional changes. In our context of studying the social model, the Lisbon Process launched in 2000 was to be a crossroads (Janssen 2005). The Lisbon Process targeted the ambitious goal of making the EU the most competitive region globally.

There were therefore at least two important events during the spring of 2006. European political and administrative leaders discussed modes of competitiveness and robust governance in relation to such models. Their explicit focus was on the Scandinavian welfare state model and its regulatory approach to social security and on whether such a successful model that offered low socioeconomic risk and vulnerability could be applied to other member states, especially those in distress (EU program 2006). This idea motivated scholars to revisit the Nordic state-focused social model and participatory administrative tradition in a comparative perspective to determine the essential characteristics of the paths of development coming out of this model and why the model is considered successful "in the global age" (EPC 2005).

As mentioned, the EU search for an innovative social model commenced when the European Council held its meeting on March 23–24, 2000, in Lisbon and agreed to set out a new ten-year strategic goal for the European Union. The goal was to make the Union *the most competitive and dynamic knowledge-based economy in the world capable of sustainable economic growth with more and better jobs and greater social cohesion.*[2]

The Lisbon Process was launched. However, right from the start, critical voices made themselves heard, such as in "Lisbon's single size does not fit all" (Mayhew 2005), meaning that the Lisbon process from the beginning was far too fixated on economic conditions for competitiveness and taming externalities at the expense of considerations of social security and welfare.

In short, the Nordic Scandinavian model seems to offer more than a "single-size" method in the pursuit of competitiveness. The model seems to offer everything that European decision-makers are looking for: highly competitive economies in conjunction with less social inequalities and the institutionalized taming of risks and regulations for job protection (EPC 2005). In the 2000s, this rather expensive welfare state model appears to represent a multidimensional method, with the potential to generate a successful road for the development of the future EU and for (some of) its member states.

Of course, all these things are extremely complicated. European-wide multidisciplinary comparative research is required to enhance the knowledge of what happens when social models travel across borders.

Welfare State Security and Risks

As elaborated above, we may view innovation in the public sector not as accidental changes but as contextual changes. In the European context, this means that path dependence due to different territorial social models strongly influences such changes (Veggeland 2007). Another issue regarding innovation arises in close connection with this. New ways of making such changes and transcending them also occur when European social models interact across borders and trigger interpretations of new ideas that bias policy and institutional change. Interpretation theory makes explicit that there are at least two basic perspectives involved (Røvik 2007: 22–23): the interpretation may be either contextual or out of context. In the contextual case, innovation is linked to already existing social models and traditions, path dependence thus determining the norms, principles, and values (Knill 2001). In the out of context case, there is the simple copying and imitating of first- or second-order changes without taking account of domestic values, management ethics, and steering traditions.

In general, regulatory innovation[3] includes strategies for improving the management of risk and the pursuit of state legitimacy in the "risk society". Innovations in the way risk is moderated include threats to welfare, social security, labor market,

---

[2]The launch of the Lisbon Process might be seen as an economic preparation for the coming enlargements.

[3]Regulatory innovation is a dynamic part of the "regulatory state"; elaboration about the latter term.

social and human capital, gender discrimination, or otherwise, environment, economy, and national security (see Taylor-Gooby (2004)). Re-regulation, a term for new regulation that aims to reduce risk and for taming purposes, is a term often used to express regulatory innovation, for example, providing social capital through market correction or the partnership approach.

Some researchers have pointed out that the welfare state is not based on "politics against the markets," as is commonly assumed in the neoliberal Anglo-Saxon tradition, but rather on the social-democratic mixed-economy approach, that is, "politics *with* markets" (Iversen 2005:73). To this can be added the postulation "politics *by* the market," if we take into consideration how the principles of New Public Management (NPM) and market-type mechanisms (MTMs) have penetrated the traditional Scandinavian welfare state model and administrative tradition (Pollitt and Bouckaert 2004; Veggeland 2004) and constituted the current Scandinavian social model (Veggeland 2007). This change has innovatively formed and adapted social capital to a new stage of welfare state performance. The three postulations seem reasonable. We should, however, qualify them with an answer to this question: which changes to the welfare state provide greater social capital to its citizens?

It is popular to point out that the market, including global markets, interferes with the welfare state and vice versa. It is, however, obvious that this interference occurs along different paths, depending on the actual social model of the states. As mentioned in previous chapters, we have at least three general welfare state models in Europe, these linking correspondingly to the three administrative and political traditions. Let us elaborate these further.

- *The Continental welfare state model*, which is dominated by strong trade unions, is said to be of a *corporatist type* with a heavily regulated labor market. As discussed earlier, high job security and protection through industrial relations plays a key role (Koukiadis 2006). For this and other reasons, the corporatist welfare states are, in many ways, based on *politics against markets* more than other European states. Administrative rigidity and the slow process of renewing social capital hamper the corporatist Continental welfare state model. These features are not accidental, but due to traditions and developments of institutional path dependence (Knill 2001).
- *The Anglo-Saxon welfare state model*, dominated by the adoption of market-centered policies, is said to be of a *liberal type*. Liberal welfare states use MTMs and independent agencies to provide welfare services. The labor market is sparsely regulated and there is low job security and protection (EPC 2005). This welfare state model, more than others, qualifies for the notion of *politics by markets*. For innovation of social capital, the model is restricted by ideological resistance to changes from the first and second levels to the transcending third level. These relate to the basic values and principles of neoliberalism. Again, this occurs not accidentally, but is a result of biases that are historically rooted in the liberal model, and we may best view this as an institutional path-dependent development.

- *The Nordic Scandinavian universal welfare state model*, dominated by state-centered policies and high welfare expenses, is of the *universal type* (Veggeland 2016). The universal welfare states offer universal social security and job protection arrangements. Furthermore, it is a governmental responsibility to prioritize such labor market tasks as lifelong learning and the development of skills. Seen from another point of view, the Nordic postwar labor market has, however, become rather liberalized and the market-type mechanism (MTM) of outsourcing is often put to use for the provision of welfare services (OECD 2005; Veggeland 2007). This qualifies the universal welfare state model for the notion of *politics with markets*.[4] The public sector has selectively learned lessons, particularly from the Anglo-Saxon model, and in some parts of society the third-level of changes is reached, that is, innovative changes. This achievement relates to the concept of social capital, which has been renewed in the contemporary Nordic model. One example is how welfare politics has become connected to labor market politics in an innovative way. The outcome has been the great social capital of "flexicurity," i.e., interactive co-play between social security and active labor market policies, which brings flexibility to the labor market and through this competitive advantages in the global age (EPC 2005). As with the other models, the contemporary universal Nordic model of the welfare state has also taken its form due to its historical welfare state roots and institutional path dependence (Olsen 2004).

One main reason why the Nordic Scandinavian model has been receiving renewed EU attention under the auspices of the EU in crisis strategies is the belief in the social capital of flexicurity and other universal welfare state arrangements of the model (Europe's World 2005). States and regions are more than ever competing globally and are intensively engaged in political and economic measures to maintain a high employment rate while trying to keep inflation and public expenses low. It is therefore understandable that they are looking for innovative solutions (Iversen 2005; EPC 2005). Records of public budgets confirm, however over the years, that the Nordic welfare and social security costs represent a high burden on the public budget. Why, then, is this model so attractive? The answer may be very simple.

> Social capital in the Scandinavian welfare-state model creates a high level of labor productivity. The labor productivity generated through the high degree of national employment means more than just "full employment" in the Keynesian sense. It means work, training or education for everybody irrespective of social groups, gender, ages and individual differences. The pay-off of this is the ability to afford expensive social security, which in turn results in the taming of social inequality that facilitates the renewal of the social capital of flexicurity in an ascending innovative circle.

The empirically based thesis is that universal job protection and social security shape the incentives provided to workers, to both invest in particular market-attractive skills and lifelong learning and to change work and workplaces without

---

[4]Torben Iversen (2005: 73) discusses the notion of politics with markets, but explicitly does not link it to the Scandinavian welfare state. He probably also includes the Anglo-Saxon model or perhaps makes it a general notion. If so, I disagree.

personal risk. Labor market flexibility is the innovative outcome of the Nordic active labor market policies: education, lifelong learning, and kindergartens that help women's access to the labor market. Firms benefit from this flexibility and access to skills, because they are critical to competitive advantage in knowledge-intensive economies. "Firms do not develop competitive advantages *in spite of* systems of social protection but *because of* it" (Iversen 2005: 74).

The European Social Capital Trade-offs

The welfare goals of a state of course need to be paid for if they are to be realized. Social capital is an instrument that can be used to accomplish that realization. Analytically, a neoliberal perspective may view the building of social capital in modern states as being directed by three goals: low inequality, low unemployment, and low public expenses. These socioeconomic goals are linked to three distinct policy choices that are characterized by a "trilemma." This trilemma occurs because it is difficult to successfully pursue all three goals simultaneously, if there are trade-offs between them. At this point, and before elaborating this statement further, there is a need to define and distinguish the notions of a trilemma and trade-offs. For these purposes, I shall follow the work of Pollitt and Bouckaert (2004: 162).

Trade-offs arise where there are more than one desideratum or more than one problem to be alleviated and where there, as a result of this, will inevitably be a failure to attain other desiderata or different problems will worsen. This is a situation, therefore, where decision-makers are obliged to balance between different things that they very much wish to achieve, but cannot possibly have them all at the same time. Indeed, having more of one desirable thing entails having less of another. In the political world, appropriate choices are often those that essentially make the best of these unavoidable, constrained conditions through the guidance of good governance grounded on a pragmatic approach. Yet, norms, values, and traditions will affect these choices by making one set of options more preferable than another. Governments thus tend to compromise the goal that is least ideologically important to them (Weaver 1986) to maximize the others, in their struggle to retain their position of political superiority. We may take the following as an example. According to the perspective of historical institutionalism (Cini 2004a, b), if decision-makers were to engineer the use of social capital as short-term instrumental capital, then the long-term perspectives that aim for sustainability and the supremacy of good governance values are often insufficiently communicated.

Torben Iversen (2005: 146–147) has highlighted this ideological aspect of the trilemma, which arises from the challenges of the global age of keeping unemployment, inequalities, and public expenses in check—in short the ideological aspect involved in social capital trade-offs. One strategy was to deregulate labor markets to reduce the power of employee unions and to increase wage flexibility. The governments of the Anglo-Saxon tradition, the USA, the United Kingdom, New Zealand, and Australia, during the 1980s exemplified these neoliberal policies. Another strategy was to both accept the consequences for employment that result from a compressed wage structure and seek to limit disruptive effects by discouraging the entry of women into the labor market and facilitating exits from the labor market, the latter primarily through the early retirement of the elderly. This is the typical pattern of choices we find to some extent in some Continental European countries.

The final option was to accept the slow growth of employment in private service sectors, but at the same time to pursue an expansive employment strategy through expansion of public sector services to balance the effective demand in the framework of Keynes. This strategy also strove to improve the educational resources available to younger people as a policy approach toward building social capital. The social-democratic governments in the Nordic countries, where the ideological tenor favored the financing of higher public expenses by full employment and by high tax rates, often chose this option.

As we observe in this process of compromising goals and policies, social models, administrative traditions, and path dependency play essential roles in what decision-makers consider to be appropriate choices and how they implement their strategic thinking on social capital (Sverdrup 2007). We can argue that the trade-offs involved in European social capital policy have the following inconsistency.

On the one hand, creating jobs and employment in the private service sector is a positive strategy, in that it does not disturb the budgetary balance. However, this strategy has certain trade-offs: lower wages, higher non-wage costs, and the inducing of negative inequality through lowering the degree of employment in the population and thereby reducing work productivity. On the other hand, the strategy of generating service jobs in the public sector also has trade-offs, the strategy indeed pushing the limits of already constrained and overloaded budgets (OECD 2005).

Politicians in charge do have the obligation to make decisions. For social capital, they look for a European model to minimize the trade-offs, that is, to find a model for flexible job creation, for social equality, and for welfare, but all within a sustainable economy (Janssen 2005; Rasmussen Nyrup 2005). The overall goal was and is to make Europe the most competitive region in the world, as was announced at the Lisbon summit meeting in 2000.[5] But the trade-offs in social capital certainly challenge this goal.

European Traditions of Governance and Trade-offs

In our context, we may briefly describe the trade-offs of equality employment and public expenses of the European welfare state models and paths in the framework of innovative social capital as the following (Veggeland 2007).

---

[5]The Lisbon summit meeting announcement; also the conditions for participating in the European Monetary Union require the economic sustainability of the member states.

- *The trade-offs in the liberal welfare state model*: As pointed out before, the Anglo-Saxon administrative tradition weighs market solutions and regulatory measures and has the lessening of state intervention as an explicitly expressed objective for the service sector. Universal welfare and health coverage are not guaranteed. The employer provides the workers' health and social insurance, while the government covers the health expenses for the poor and the elderly who fall outside this insurance system.

  – In this tradition, the response to the equality employment trade-offs was to give job creation and labor market flexibility priority while reducing job protection and social security. The use of worker contracting reduced the power of unions and increased wage inequality during the 1980s. Politicians and economists believed in a flexible labor market that would make full use of the economic capacity and promote job creation, innovation, and growth through a flexible labor market, without fixed tariffs and expensive welfare services. The engineering of short-term social capital was part of this belief. For neoliberal economists, market flexibility is the ultimate precondition and solution for increasing productivity and revitalizing the European economy in a globally competitive world.

- *The trade-offs in the Corporatist welfare state*: The Continental administrative tradition depends on corporative solutions and state-interventionist measures. Health and social insurance are guaranteed, although the latter is a mixture of public and private institutional arrangements. Traditional welfare services are kept in the public domain as "services of general interest." Trade unions are strong, but too few jobs are, as a result of this, created. Reaching Hall's third-level institutional change did not, then, come fast enough.

  – In this tradition, the response to the equality employment trade-offs was to accept the employment consequences of a formal wage structure and hierarchical and rigid system of professionals, the latter also dominating the bargaining area. The labor market remained inflexible and the unemployment rate relatively high. Policies for social capital building did not stand up to solutions that obstinately remained "policies against the market."

- *The trade-offs in the Universal Scandinavian welfare state*: The Nordic Scandinavian administrative tradition relies on public institutional solutions for social equality, interventionist measures, universal welfare services, and public health and social insurance arrangements as goals and means for the building of social capital (Veggeland 2016). Institutional changes at Hall's three levels have created public innovations. The use of MTM in the public sector, such as in outsourcing and contracting out arrangements and the selective reorganization of public administration to public-law agencies (PLAs) and private-law bodies (PLBs), has led to indirect governance by regulation becoming common, and trade union power diminishing since the 1980s (OECD 2002; Veggeland 2007, 2004).

– In this tradition, the response to the equality employment trade-offs was to accept sluggish employment growth in private services while expanding the public service sector and public expenses, resulting in high taxes. The influence of professionals in the main bargaining arena was limited, because Nordic unions, unlike unions in countries such as Germany and France, were sharply divided between blue- and white-collar workers. The governments also took anticipatory measures for building human capital, such as lifelong learning, adult education, and continuous training, to adjust skills to the changing needs in both the private and public sectors. Close to 20% of all adults (those between the ages of 25 and 65) participate in some kind of adult education every year, compared with an average of around 8% for the EU as a whole. A rather flexible labor market has developed as a result of the implementation of this concept of social capital. The payoff in terms of the universal welfare state facilitates the general acceptance of the relatively high tax level.

Conclusions

The Scandinavian countries have a long shared history and have experienced similar and common social and economic developments. The most common feature of their systems is a well-developed welfare state characterized by its universalism, meaning that all citizens are entitled to basic social benefits and job protection and that there is high social spending, high taxes, and a large public sector. They have succeeded in achieving a high degree of labor market flexibility and are close to fulfilling one of the goals of the Lisbon Process of an overall employment rate of 70%.

Employment policies lie at the heart of the Nordic countries' labor market policy, just as social security policies lie at the heart of their welfare state policy. The framework of the two policies is innovation and long-term social capital building, such as flexicurity. Obviously, these policies pay off only when they are associated with low inequality and high public welfare expenses and employment.

Even if they did not initiate the Lisbon Strategy, the Nordic EU member countries are very comfortable with it, particularly its initial triple focus on the labor market, employment, and social inclusion in a knowledge-based economy and under regulatory governance (Europe's World 2005). The similarity between the priorities of the Lisbon Process and the past and current actions of social capital building in the Nordic countries have, however, led some to ask whether the Lisbon reform agenda was simply an ambitious attempt by these countries to position their welfare state policy in line *"with the market."* The flexicurity model has firmly influenced European economic and social models (Janssen 2005).

This interpretation is, however, unlikely to be the case. The launching of the process of comprehensive renewal by the participants in Lisbon in 2000 represented a collective recognition of the challenges the EU faces and the need for a common response that would be able to draw on the best elements and paths of each member state's social and economic models and administrative traditions. This means a consensus across different models, rather than the imposition of one single approach to all. Indeed, some feared that the Lisbon Reforms would represent the introduction of a divisive Anglo-Saxon model, far from a Scandinavian one, and would then be only partially successful. This fear led to unjustified concerns that the actual agenda for growth and jobs would disastrously lead to high inequality, that is, less social protection and the undermining of the role of the state. There was also the fear that the standards applied to the smaller countries were not always applied to the large countries. In the wake of discussions, conflicting areas emerged.

References

Amin, A. (Ed.). (1994). *Post-Fordism: A reader*. Cambridge: Blackwell.
Anderson, P. (1994). *The invention of the region, 1945–1990* (EUI Working Paper 94(2)). Florence: EUF.
Austvik, O. G. (2002). *Internasjonal handel og økonomisk integrasjon*. Oslo: Gyldendal Akademisk.
Brunsson, N. (2011). *The organization of hypocrisy*. Copenhagen: Liber.
Castells, M. (1996). *The rise of the network society*. Oxford: Blackwell.
Cini, M. (Ed.). (2004a). *European Union politics*. Oxford: Oxford University Press.
Cini, M. (2004b). Intergovernmentalism. In M. Cini (Ed.), *European Union politics*. Oxford: Oxford University Press.
Dahl-Eriksen, T. (1997). *Suverene stater og transnasjonale regioner* [Sovereign states and transnational regions] (HiF-rapport nr. 6//1997). Alta.
de Buck, P. (2004). The social dialogue and the role of social partners in the EEA. *EFTA Bulletin*, 73–78. Brussels: EFTA.
EPC Working Paper. (2005). *The Nordic model: A recipe for European success?* (Working Paper 20). European Policy Centre.
Europe's World. (2005, Autumn). *The Only Europe-Wide Policy Journal*.
Haas, E. B. (1958). *The uniting of Europe: Political, social and economic forces – 1950–1957*. Stanford, CA: Stanford University Press.
Hoffmann, S. (1996). Obstinate or obsolete? The fate of the nation-state and the case of Western Europe. *Daedalus, 95*(3), 862–915.
Iversen, T. (2005). *Capitalism: Democracy and welfare*. Cambridge: Cambridge University Press.
Janssen, D. (2005, Autumn). Retreat or Relaunch: Choices for the Lisbon agenda, in Europe's World. *The Only Europe-wide Policy Journal, 1*, 54–57.
Keating, M., & Loughlin, J. (Eds.). (1997). *The political economy of regionalism*. London: Frank Cass.
Keohane, R. O., & Nye, J. S. (1977). *Power and independence: World politics in transition*. Boston, MA: Little Brown and Company.
Knill, C. (2001). *The Europeanization of the national administrations*. Cambridge: Cambridge University Press.
Koukiadis, I. D. (2006). *The imminent retirement of socialism and the hope of a new social state*. Athens: The Epitheorisi Ergasiakon Scheseon.
Krasner, S. (1983). Structural causes and regime consequences, regimes as intervening variables. In S. Krasner (Ed.), *International regimes*. London: Cornell University Press.
March, J. & Olsen, J. P. (2005). *The institutional dynamics of international political order* (Arena Working Papers 98/5). Oslo: University of Oslo.

Mayhew, A. (2005). Lisbon's single size doesn't fit all, *Europe's World*, Autumn edition.

Millward, A. S. (2000). *The European rescue of the nation-state*. London: Routledge.

Moravcsik, A. (1993). Preferences and power in the European Community: A liberal intergovernmentalist approach. *Journal of Common Market Studies, 2*(2), 226–249.

Moravcsik, A. (1998). *The choice of Europe: Social purpose and state power from Messina to Maastricht*. London: University College London Press.

Nye, J. S. (2004). *Soft power: The means to success in world politics*. New York: Public Affairs.

Nye, J. S. (1971). Comparing common markets: A revised neo-functional model. In L. N. Lindberg & S. A. Scheingold (Eds.), *Regional integration: Theory and research*. Cambridge: Cambridge University Press.

OECD. (2002). *Distributed public governance: Agencies, authorities and other government bodies*. Paris: OECD.

OECD. (2005). *Modernising government: The way forward*. Paris: OECD.

Olsen, J. P. (2005). *Maybe it is time to rediscover bureaucracy?* (Working Paper 10). Oslo: Arena University of Oslo.

Olsen, J. P. (2004). Europeanization. In M. Cini (Ed.), *European Union politics* (pp. 333–348). Oxford: Oxford University Press.

Pollack, M. A. (2005). Theorizing EU policy-making. In H. Wallace, W. Wallace, & M. A. Polack (Eds.), *Policy-making in the European Union* (pp. 13–48). Oxford: Oxford University Press.

Pollitt, C., & Bouckaert, G. (2004). *Public management reform: A comparative analysis*. Oxford: Oxford University Press.

Rasmussen Nyrup, P. (2005, Autumn). What Lisbon has cached is political courage. *Europe's World*, 60–70.

Rosamond, B. (2000). *Theories of European integration*. London: MacMillan Press.

Røvik, K. A. (2007). *Translasjoner og Trender. Ideer som former det 21. århundrets organisasjon (Translations and Trends. Ideas that shape the 21st century)*. Bergen: Fagbokforlaget.

Strøby Jensen, C. (2004). Neo-functionalism. In M. Cini (Ed.), *European Union politics* (pp. 80–92). Oxford: Oxford University Press.

Sverdrup, U. (2007). Implementation. In P. Graziano & M. P. Vink (Eds.), *Europeanization: New Research Agendas*. Basingstoke: Palgrave MacMillan.

Taylor-Gooby, P. (Ed.). (2004). *New risks, new welfare: The transformation of European Welfare State*. Oxford: Oxford University Press.

Tinbergen, J. (1965). *International economic integration*. Amsterdam: Elsevier.

Urwin, D. W. (1996). *The community of Europe: The history of European integration since 1945*. London: Longman.

Veggeland, N. (2004). *The competitive society: How democratic and effective?* Kristiansand: Norwegian Academic Press.

Veggeland, N. (2007). *Paths of public innovation in the Global age: Lessons from Scandinavia*. Northampton, MA: Edward Elgar.

Veggeland, N. (2013). *Essays on regulatory governance*. New York: Nova Science.

Veggeland, N. (Ed.). (2016). *The current Nordic welfare state model*. New York: Nova Science.

Veggeland, N. (Ed.). (2017). *Administrative strategies of our time*. New York: Nova Science.

Weaver, R. K. (1986). The politics of blame avoidance. *Journal of Public Policy, 6*(4), 371–398.

Chapter 8
Conflicting Economic Politics

Introduction

Keynesianism is a national focused macroeconomic theory (Veggeland 2018), Keynesian theory building on the assumption that prices and wages are sticky, leading to imbalance, high inflation, or deflation. This, in combination with various market crises such as the current financial crisis, suggests that the market always fails to achieve full employment and fails to avoid crises that affect unemployment. Thus, Keynesians argue that active state stabilization and labor market policy in the form of fiscal and monetary policies can create just and full employment and good business, while market deregulation and laissez-faire policies fail (Woolner 2018).

Left Side Policy

Canada, with Justin Trudeau as prime minister and with social democratic politics, overcame the Liberal Party in the autumn of 2015. The party won with clearly stated neo-Keynesian rhetoric and an emphasis on the state's importance as a basis for its reform proposals for the revival of the welfare state, after its destruction by the conservative government. In the USA, the socialist/Social Democrat Senator Bernard "Bernie" Sanders emerged as a popular democratic opposition candidate to Hillary Clinton. In the United Kingdom, we see the same thing happening with the British variety of labor in opposition, the Social Democratic British Labour Party. The selection of Socialist Jeremy Corbyn as party leader shows a completely new turn to the left. In Spain, Portugal, Italy, and Greece, we also see the same shift to the left. In Greece, Syriza won the elections and is in a government position. A Scandinavian example of Norwegian social democracy is shown in the Norwegian Labor Party. The party has not yet followed this political turn to the left, but has made efforts to maintain the support of the right liberal political center around the

© Springer Nature Switzerland AG 2020
N. Veggeland, *Democratic Governance in Scandinavia*,
https://doi.org/10.1007/978-3-030-18270-0_8

Christian Democrats, to gain power in the general Parliamentary election of September 2017. The Labor Party became, in the election, a political loser, winning fewer votes than in the 2013 election. On the other hand, the Labor Party is still Norway's largest political party measured in terms of votes. In 2019, it is the more left-wing political parties that are, according to the polls, growing in popularity in Norway.

Neo-Keynesianism

The reasons for this are many. One obvious reason is, however, that Norwegian social democracy still lacks a basic economic alternative to the anti-statist neoclassical economic theory and policy ideology that manifests as the neoliberalism of today. Countering this theory and policy today is a theory and policy approach referred to as neo-Keynesian (Krugman 2007). This policy approach is, for social democracy, an option. As the name suggests, it builds on Keynes's momentous theory from 70 years ago (Woolner 2018).

One of the main elements of John Maynard Keynes' theory, *General Theory of Employment, Interest and Money* of 1936, was in response to the interwar depression and employment crisis. This element defined the need for states, in times of crisis, to "fill the hole" in overall demand, in particular the demand for labor. In the 1930s, one-third of the workforce was available for work in Norway. Keynes' theory formed the basis for Norwegian Keynesian policy in the postwar years and the goal of full employment, which was achieved. Keynes pointed out that effective demand must be achieved by the government spending more money than it collects in tax revenues. This leads to a public deficit in a period without provisions. However, the damaging effect of this is surpassed as the employment rate increases, so increasing value creation.

A new Keynesianism, based on the classic Keynesian theory, stresses the need for increased governmental, institutional, and economic interventions as unemployment rises and national and international recessions gain traction. The classic variant, designed for national policy, is neo-Keynesianism. This also targets international crisis measures such as actions under the auspices of the EU and its Central Bank (ECB) (see Binder 2004). See also Keynesian Economics (2017).

Under the classic Keynesian models, government intervention is intended to spur the long-term changes that result from a period of national stagnation. These are, in an economic recession, intended to create a macroeconomic balance between supply and demand through the help of the government. Keynes focused on the large cyclical fluctuations of capitalism, not the microeconomic fluctuations at the institutional and enterprise level, an approach emphasized by neo-Keynesianism. The government's countercyclical policy adopted by the USA was inspired by neo-Keynesian thinking (Skidelsky 2009). When the financial crisis came in 2007, unemployment rose to more than 10% and the federal government granted the staggering sum of $800 trillion dollars to stimulus and demand measures. The goal was to create macro- and microeconomic demand, to reverse the trend back toward normal economic growth. In 2016 and as a result of this governmental intervention, unemployment was just over 5%.

Job Creation by State Intervention

According to the neo-Keynesian approach, both short-term and long-term government investments are involved in activities aimed at job creation. This approach has unintentionally influenced the Norwegian social democratic opposition in the Parliament. The opposition's response to today's economic stagnation caused by the crisis in the Norwegian oil and gas sector, the migration crisis, and rapidly growing unemployment is to demand that the government immediately initiates actions such as the development of public sector jobs and emergency work such as the plugging of disused oil wells in the North Sea. "Dig a hole" in the ground to create employment, wrote Keynes in his theory. The incumbent government was characterized, however, by inaction to rising unemployment and the hope that the market would settle with private entrepreneurs leading the way.

Neo-Keynesians strongly refute austerity measures as precautions in the public sector and government inaction to a recession and rising unemployment. Tightening will result in further unemployment and so a vicious circle. They furthermore argue that reducing bank interest rates to zero does not help economic stagnation in the short term. The lack of demand in the economy, both nationally and internationally, prevents borrowing and investment irrespective of interest rates. The use of tax policy and the reduction of tax to increase investment is not an effective instrument, for the same reason, they pointed out (Nilsson 2018).

Nobel Prize Winners

The two American Nobel Prize winners in economics, Joseph Stiglitz (b. 1943) and Paul Krugman (b. 1953), are the most famous exponents of the neo-Keynesian economic theory of our time. This is a theory of political diversions in the combating of the negative effects of crisis and recession. These two economists represent the highest level of academic prestige. They are read and cited. Their theory has, however, been partially rejected by those with political power in the EU and Europe. The rejection has been clearly shown in their published counterargument to the austerity measures imposed by the EU and IMF on distressed countries such as Greece. These counterarguments have been ignored. Now it seems that the vision of the EU with respect to the importance of governmental tools and interventions will change in the wake of the refugee and migration crisis. The return of Keynesian policies in a new form, with a government-friendly international solidarity perspective, is also obviously accompanied by neoliberalism being on the verge of collapse in Europe due to the ongoing financial crisis, the euro crisis, and the refugee crisis.

Joseph Stiglitz wrote in 2010 *Freefall: America, Free Markets, and Sinking of the World Economy* and Paul Krugman wrote in 2010 "Keynes Who?" They currently are in the process of adopting the same critical but central role played by the economist John Maynard Keynes. In the postwar years, they are in the position of creating a theoretical basis for a political way out of the financial crisis of 2007. Keynes reacted to the deep international economic depression, culminating in 1929 and subsequent years. Keynes theories were caught by European social democrats, such as the Norwegian Labor Party, which implemented the successful policy of the first decades after World War II. The policy was built in an active state of state, institutional, and economic interventions, social cohesion, and increased public spending. For Keynes, this was necessary if a capitalist economy in crisis was to restore and preserve long-term aggregate effective demand and purchasing power, full employment being a goal. How could both unemployment and inflation be established at a low and stable level? The development of the Norwegian Keynesian welfare state in the postwar years of universal rights, politically led by the social democracy of the Labor Party, was an important element in the policy of maintaining stable effective demand in the economy as a whole. Social democracy could then realize its ideas of social and economic cohesion and justice (Nyseter 2015).

Neoclassical liberal economic policies, with an emphasis on public austerity, small government, and privatization, dominated prior to Keynes, small state and market liberalization being believed to cure the 1920s and 1930s economic recession. Keynes and his theories of an active state initially gained little attention, because of his strong disagreement with the classical liberal economic theory of policy tightening and a shrinking state. In our time, we correspondingly see tightening and privatization policy as being a response to the EU/EEA area's financial crisis (which Norway is a part) and Eurozone debt crisis. The negative impact of this tightening and privatization policy is most clearly seen in crisis-hit Greece and other Mediterranean countries. In Norway, the blue government neoliberal approach to the problem of rising unemployment and migration crisis is being pushed in the direction of public austerity and privatization, based on the blue government's neoliberal ideological stance and policy background.

Stiglitz and Krugman are, in the international orthodox neoclassical setting, given as little attention as Keynes originally was. The practical reforms that logically follow their neo-Keynesian ideas and theories have, seen from a neoliberal perspective, sometimes had drastic consequences. This would mean the liquidation of the privatization program and the return of privatized physical infrastructure such as railways, water, and telecommunications and social infrastructures such as kindergartens, schools, and care to the state as owner and operator. It would also mean extensive regulation of the financial sector, tax reforms, and financial transfers, the aim being social cohesion for greater purchasing power and justice and ultimately the possible increase in public spending as an intended consequence.

Neo-Keynesian Confrontation with the Neoliberals

The primary disagreement between new classical liberal and neo-Keynesian economists, with Stiglitz and Krugman as spokesmen of the neo-Keynesian approach, is how quickly do price and income (purchasing power) align in the market? Neoclassical economists assume that this takes place in a flexible way, supply and demand balancing by themselves (invisible hand) and without unemployment and inflation occurring. New Keynesian economists reject this assumption and argue that this balance cannot alone improve the market, but that state interventions and regulations must politically ensure purchasing power, effective demand, and full employment. If this is not carried out, then inflation-fueled inflation, in parallel with a declining purchasing power in terms of unemployment and the social dumping of employment and poverty, will result. A negative downward spiral ensues. The consequence will be the socioeconomic crisis we see in Europe today, with declining investment, high unemployment, and social deprivation in many countries.

A theory and policy alternative to neoliberalism's theoretical foundation is the social democracy of today. This option, located in the central state-focused neo-Keynesian macroeconomic approach, now wins the vote in opposition politics in Anglo-American countries and Mediterranean countries in crisis. In Norway, social democracy in the opposition's neo-Keynesian policy is believed to fit their ideology and rhetoric in the election in 2017 (Veggeland 2018).

The Norwegian Case

Market liberalism also entered into the political realities of Norway in the 1980s. Today's right-wing government is confident in its belief in neoliberalism and in leading active and unilateral policies for deregulated free markets and the marketization of public services. The tightening welfare state and tax cuts provided to the wealthiest are contrary to the Keynesian principle of social and economic cohesion and are justified for example by the preservation of purchasing power and effective demand. The social democratic coalition government policy between 2005 and 2013 was also based on (light) neoliberalism. Norwegian Social Democracy retrieves a foundation in the new Keynesian economic theory and policy, as classical Keynesianism did in the decades after World War II.

Norway is fortunate and does not need Keynesian deficits to create effective demand and new jobs. Norway has an oil fund, the Government "Pension Fund—abroad" with a market capitalization of 8500 billion and which invests in 9000 companies in 75 countries worldwide. Government money from the oil fund today goes partly to the unnecessary privatization of public welfare services, which is costing billions. Extended outsourcing, which monopolizes all operations from receipt, settlement, language training, and employment services to private businesses, is now normal. This is gaining ground, as monopolists push up prices, the state paying for this and few stable employment gains resulting from the unreasonable expenditures. The government oil fund is otherwise used to compensate for tax cuts in the state budget and as a long-term strategy for job creation. This is a passive misuse that research shows has little effect on economic growth and increased job creation (More 2014).

In Norway, job creation processes have been renationalized in line with a neo-Keynesian guide. The state must be an active investor in new government jobs in welfare sectors such as health care, education, and training, and in business, as reflected by the Keynesian approach. Only then will it be possible to employ the new hundred thousand migrants, plus the second hundred thousand nonmigrant unemployed, as was achieved with Keynes' help in the economic depression between the wars. The establishment of state enterprises must no longer be a taboo strategy. In an era of the green turning of economic production in the direction of new international markets, Norway can be a pioneer of a profitable, sustainable job creation policy, the migration crisis and growing unemployment being the starting point. Such a policy will again provide content for the rhetorical concepts required for the restructuring of and innovation within the Norwegian economy.

Short Summary

Refuting the neoliberal orthodoxy turns out not to be easy. We, however, see such a trend in Western capitalist countries seeking neo-Keynesian solutions. When the feudal system of the monarchy, the church, and the nobility was brought to its knees in Europe 250 years ago, an economic and political ideology directed against all monopoly power emerged, it also rejecting strong state power. This ideology coined the well-known name of market liberalism. Its roots were classical economic theory from the seventeenth and eighteenth centuries. Just as rabbits conquered every corner of the Australian continent after introduction, so market liberalism gnawed down and soon spread to all the earth's cardinal points. The successor, neoliberalism, is the dominant ideology of the Western capitalist countries of today. Neo-Keynesianism and its state-friendly theoretical approach to economic stability and job creation has picked up its gloves to fight neoliberal socioeconomic policy solutions and, so far, to some extent has won in some countries such as Canada. On the other hand, the case of the traditionally social democratic ruling system of Norway shows that the ideology of neoliberalism has taken over dominance among citizens and political parties.

Further research can be conducted to find out more about the confrontation between neoliberalism and neo-Keynesianism, which today is playing out their rhetoric and policies in the realm of nations and societies. This means giving priority to comparative empirical studies and case studies that can reveal processes and power constellations.

References

Binder, A. S. (2004). *The quiet revolution*. New Haven, CT: Yale University Press.

Keynes, J. M. (1936). *The general theory of employment, interest and money*. London: Macmillan.

Keynesian Economics. (2017). *The concise encyclopedia of economics*. Princeton, NJ: Princeton University Press.

Krugman, P. (2007). *The conscience of a liberal*. Princeton, NJ: Princeton University Press.

More, M. C. (2014). *Tax and spend: The welfare state, tax politics and the limit of American liberalism*. Philadelphia, PA: Pennsylvania University Press.

Nilsson, J. E. (2018). New Keynesian policy: The revival of each policy maker's dream. In N. Veggeland (Ed.), *The Keynesian policies – A new deal in the European narrative. Employment, equality and sustainability*. New York: Nova Science.

Nyseter, T. (2015). *Velferd på avveie: Reformer, verdier, veivalg*. Oslo: Res Publica.

Skidelsky, R. (2009). *Keynes: The return of the master*. New York: Public Affairs.

Stiglitz, J. (2010). *Freefall: America, free markets, and sinking of the world economy*. New York: W. W. Norton.

Veggeland, N. (Ed.). (2018). *The Keynesian policies – A new deal in the European Narrative. Employment, equality and sustainability*. New York: Nova Science.

Woolner, D. B. (2018). Franklin D. Roosevelt: The Reluctant Keynesian. In N. Veggeland (Ed.), *Keynesian policies – A new deal in the European narrative. Employment, equality and sustainability*. New York: Nova Science.

Chapter 9
Case Study: Accounting Reform—In Regulatory Norway

Introduction

Accounting is based on revenues and expenditures. Revenues represent cash receipt claims that are due either immediately or at some date in the future. Expenditures represent obligations to make cash payments, immediately or at a point in the future. The budget of net budgeting in the public sector should be balanced at the end of the budget period. The focus is on the money effect in the sense that a budgeted activity is maintained and developed during this period. Public sector budgets show expenditures (payroll, schools, public assistance, health care, roads) and how they are to be financed in the form of revenues (tax revenues, duties). Traditional budgets, however, represent an expenditure and revenue budget, or a money budget in other words.

Business accounts focus on the profitability effect of revenues and expenditures. The profitability effect refers to profitability in the form of revenues (accrued revenues) and profitability in the form of expenditures (investments). This entails two-dimensional accrual accounting. A profitability accrual principle is added to the money accrual principle. The first-mentioned principle, often referred to imprecisely as the accrual principle, is used to report the profitability effect of both revenues and expenditures (Monsen 2009).

The selection of an accounting model for use in the public sector has traditionally been based on a political desire that is linked to the right and the opportunity to govern. The introduction of business-oriented accounting in the public sector has, however, weakened this opportunity to govern. Why has this reform therefore been implemented? Norvald Monsen (2009) suggests the following answers in an article on accounting in the public sector:

1. "There is a political perception that the public sector should be governed to the greatest possible extent like the private sector, and thus there is a need to prepare the same accounts that are prepared in the private sector (business accounts in other words).

© Springer Nature Switzerland AG 2020
N. Veggeland, *Democratic Governance in Scandinavia*,
https://doi.org/10.1007/978-3-030-18270-0_9

2. Insufficient knowledge of what business accounts represent.
3. Insufficient knowledge of the alternatives that exist for business accounts."

Let us take a closer look at business-oriented accounting in the public sector, its origins, its implementation, and its consequences.

Accounting can be perceived as a neutral tool for budgetary control. But it is not. What may look like technical functions, such as bookkeeping and liquidity management, are, beyond the purely technical aspects, guidelines for political assessments and how the administration of public services takes place. They trigger growth in the so-called measurement bureaucracy (Veggeland 2009).

Business operations are furthermore closely tied to the realization of profits. This, in itself, is irrelevant in the public sector, which bases its activities and budgets on taxpayers' money. It is important to understand that the model for business-oriented accounting was not developed in Norway. It is based on an international standard, the International Public Sector Accounting Standards (IPSAS), which originated in the early 1990s (www.ipsas.org/). This standard was created in the Anglo-Saxon tradition of public administration (the United Kingdom, the USA, New Zealand, Australia), which was business-oriented at its core. The standards spread to a number of other Western countries, including those in southern Europe, the consequences of this for these countries' economies in the late 2000s being a deep-seated economic and social crisis. In accordance with IPSAS, revenues are recorded in the budget period in which they are earned, regardless of when they are received. The same holds true for expenses. They are also recorded in the period they are incurred, irrespective of whether they have been paid (Deaconu et al. 2011). The profitability accrual principle is that which applies.

The Difficult Financial Control

This creates ambiguity in the budgets of public institutions and makes financial control difficult, for example, in unit price financing of patients in the health services and students at universities and university colleges. The timing of revenues and total expenses often does not correspond. When, for example, students are admitted to a study program, they are recorded as an expense. The revenues however and in accordance with unit price financing are accrued 2 years after students graduate. In this way, an apparent "deficit" is created. On the other hand, if the number of students declines in a period (due to failing to graduate), then a genuine deficit occurs. In the hospital sector, patients may be released too early because, from an economic perspective, the readmission of these same patients would be recorded as new revenue in the hospital accounts, as defined by the unit price system. The Coordination Reform, i.e., the agreement between the municipalities and health trusts on the transfer of patients whose treatment is completed to the municipalities, may reinforce the tendency to release patients from hospitals too early. The price set for each student and each patient is often arbitrary, and in the public sector, one cannot rely on demand in the market for price information.

Business-oriented accounting has a number of other consequences that affect the political and social order. One of these is that it pressures society to move toward a greater degree of privatization and the competitive tendering of public services. A major reason for this is the problem of pricing public assets, such as public property: buildings, land, furnishings, technical equipment, and infrastructure. Should these be priced according to their market value or their value to society and the community? Value-based pricing tends to be based on the present value of the capital assets and cash flow and does not incorporate changes over time. The price is usually too high and arbitrary (Newberry 2012).

The result of most assets being usually priced too high is that, from an accounting perspective, the services produced in public enterprises are found not to be competitive with services produced in private companies. This becomes a driving force toward more privatization and competitive tendering in the public sector, as a result of the political guidelines of the accounting system.

Another consequence is that politicians must almost be experts in analyzing financial statements to understand the information in the accounts. Even experienced economists and top-level managers can find it difficult to follow changes in assets and budget accruals, expenses being recorded in 1 year and revenues maybe not being recorded until several years later. What happens in the interim when pricing does not occur in a fluid market, but in the public sector?

Sue Newberry (2012), a researcher in this field, gives an example of similar problems in New Zealand. In 2005, it was discovered that the authorities had sold a public electrical power plant that had been recorded according to business-oriented accounting principles. However, the accounts also showed that the very same power plant was leased back from an owner in a tax haven. There was no debate about this, as it was difficult to see it in the accounts. When it was discovered, it was too late to reverse the sale. In general, Newberry cautions against using business-oriented accounting and urges Western European countries such as Norway to learn from New Zealand's mistake. New Zealand has reversed the trend toward management by objectives and results (which has a monopolizing effect) and the trend toward business-oriented accounting.

The Norwegian Case

Politicians and employees in the public sector do not necessarily have a background in private business. This is why they often find it difficult to understand business-oriented accounting. This creates a democratic problem, because politicians, institutional leaders, and inspectorates are often placed in a position of powerlessness (Newberry and Pallot 2006).

Business management is known from the organizationally independent public enterprises and companies in Norway. It has, however, been implemented in such diverse areas as hospitals, postal services, railways, roads, telecommunications, and electrical power, and in ordinary public institutions (such as universities and university colleges).

The Norwegian Government Agency for Financial Management was established on January 1, 2004, under the Ministry of Finance and was charged with responsibility for the administration of regulations for business-oriented accounting. In 2011, the Norwegian name of the agency was changed from *Senter for statlig økonomi (SSØ)* to *Direktoratet for økonomistyring (DFØ)*. The DFØ is the government's expert body on financial management within public sector activities. The overall objective of the directorate is to facilitate suitable common solutions within the state and effective management in public enterprises. The directorate seeks to promote the efficient use of resources in the state through business-oriented accounting systems. This is to be accomplished through training measures, advisory services, and the development of methods and tools, accounting services being delivered to about 60% of public enterprises. The DFØ is responsible for the state's accounts and the state's cash pool.

As a regulatory body, the DFØ seeks to counteract the negative effects of an increasingly fragmented state that uses many different accounting forms. The Ministry of Finance, however, cautions that: "The SSØ must balance consideration for direct profits through standardized common solutions with the need for customized solutions in the individual public enterprises" (Ministry of Finance 2009: 2). This is where risk assessment and risk management come into play. The concept of vulnerability is integrated into general risk theory.

Vulnerability may, in this context, be understood as combining business management and uncertainty with respect to a balanced budget. That the system is vulnerable is also taken for granted. This means, in practice, that accrual-based business-oriented accounting should not be viewed just on the basis of the current situation but also on the basis of complex conditions in the past and future. It is the task of the DFØ to assist institutions with this.

Part of the risk assessment performed by the DFØ therefore entails formulating an opinion on whether an institution that is managed according to business principles is organized in a way that allows it to respond to reasonable expectations of the services it provides. Expectations of a public service institution, such as a hospital, will encompass conditions related to internal processes and problems, as well as external conditions such as waiting lists and patients' rights.

Public institutions cost money. Internal expenses are related to operations and bureaucracy, expensive measurement and reporting activities, quality assurance in association with effective financial management, and maintaining an overview of earnings. There is a risk that an imbalance will therefore develop. A paradox arises (Veggeland 2012). Increasing internal transaction costs impacts the primary activity. The DFØ, however, coming from a completely different perspective registers good budgeting and accounting practices and effective use of public assistance schemes. Everything is, in the view of the state, working as it should. This conflict in perspectives is familiar from the health care and education sector and from other sectors. Is the state independent or just confused (Difi Report 2012)?

Universal Public Services

The DFØ may be seen as occupying a role that is primarily related to neutral technocratic consulting and further development of business-oriented accounting as an instrument of management. This view is too simplistic, because the agency's task is carried out within the neoliberal framework of the regulatory state (Majone 1994; Veggeland 2010). The DFØ's activities and the new forms of management and business-oriented accounting in the public sector must be seen as a key component of New Public Management (NPM). Yet, NPM reforms have been implemented on the basis of clear international ideological and political principles (Lane 2000; Kjær 2004).

We are familiar with NPM reforms as being the basis of organizational autonomy and the establishment of public enterprises and companies in Norway. Reforms were implemented in areas such as hospitals, postal services, railways, roads, telecommunications, and power plants. Enterprises and companies became separate legal entities and their accounts became business driven. Experience, as we have seen, shows that this form of management is not unproblematic. Nor is it possible to determine which public services are beneficial to society as a whole and which are "commercially viable." Which perspective should be used? It is extremely difficult to define commercial viability, since public services are universal in nature. That is, they are supposed to be available to everyone and independent of the market. For example, how can the commercial value of the health care sector be determined? Or of social welfare schemes? Or of education? There has, however, been an attempt to do precisely this by converting social welfare and education into capital and economic value. We are familiar with terms such as social capital, human resource capital, and knowledge-based economy (Putnam 1993; Navarro 2002). Such capital quantities for social welfare and education can, in translation, be accounted for as commercial contributions on the revenue side based on a complex and approximate calculation.

Historical Roots

The business model has historical roots. As we have seen, the model washed over the OECD's member states as a result of the international financial crisis that arose in the mid-1970s. In the 1980s, globalization, liberalization, and the creation of new markets generated a need for greater national competitiveness and innovation in order to come out of the crisis. The Anglo-Saxon countries were leaders in this.

The idea arose of also bringing public enterprises in as commercial actors in the market to increase Norway's competitiveness in a situation of tight national budgets. According to this ideology, only the use of business management principles and competitive tendering could make public enterprises innovative and thus productive in a national economic sense (Veggeland 2012). The model, however, required extensive reforms to be applied in Norway. These were implemented in the 1990s and into the 2000s, followed by the introduction of business-oriented accounting. The SSØ/DFØ was established in 2004 as a continuation of the strategies chosen and implemented in the 1990s.

The establishment of the SSØ/DFØ and the agency's focus on financial management must be seen in the light of the extensive market orientation in the public sector in general. The Norwegian Government in the early 2000s, headed by the right-wing Prime Minister Kjell-Magne Bondevik, was so fixated on a market-oriented approach that it stated in its introduction to the new competition legislation at the time that competition and financial management should not only be a tool for enhancing efficiency, but "a goal in itself." The recommendation for the Act, which entered into force on May 1, 2004, states: "This means that competition must be given special consideration within all political areas and that competition must be an independent goal on par with other considerations in society" (Ministry of Labor and Government Administration 2003: 6). In this context, the same government established the SSØ/DFØ, from this perspective a regulatory body charged with the task of creating a rational, business-oriented approach through competition in a fragmented state created by the establishment of state enterprises. DFØ's mandate indicates such a goal. The political belief in business management and its link to competition, unit price financing, and accounting as applied to welfare services such as health care, child protection, public communication, and education can be difficult to understand. The DFØ also noted, on several occasions, that this can be difficult. Its response was, however, usually: although not everything can be measured, why not measure what can be measured with a view to business management, based on rational economic principles? This is one of the key pillars of the new forms of public sector management that the DFØ, a regulatory and advisory agency, represents.

Social Implications

Studies show that the narrow business-oriented focus in the public sector undermines the motivation of many people who work as service providers in the sector. They experience stress from planning activities, efficiency indicator measurements, reporting requirements, reams of forms, internal invoicing, calls for tenders, and continual organizational changes aimed at enhancing cost efficiency. This, ultimately, also affects the users of the services. Paradoxically an enterprise can, despite these negative consequences, appear to excel in financial management, such as shown in statistical tables and comparisons. A key question can therefore be asked and has been asked by organizational theorists: is it not perhaps time to resurrect traditional organizational forms and accounting procedures? This is what has occurred in countries such as New Zealand (Newberry 2012). For the DFØ, this could mean that the agency must change its name to the "Government Agency for Social Management," meaning that it would be charged with a new, broader mandate with an emphasis on "other considerations," i.e., nonmeasurable values in the welfare state that are not identified in a purely business-oriented perspective.

References

Deaconu, A., Nistor, C. S., & Filip, C. (2011). The impact of accrual accounting on public sector management. An exploratory study for Romania. *Transylvanian Review of Administrative Sciences, 32*(E/2011), 74–97.
Difi Report. (2012). *Difi-rapport nr 7, Uavhengig eller bare uavklart? Organisering av statlig myndighetsutøvelse*. Oslo: Oslo-dep.
Kjær, A. M. (2004). *Governance*. Malden, MA: Polity.
Lane, J. E. (2000). *New public management*. London: Routledge.
Majone, G. (1994). The rise of the regulatory state in Europe. *West European Politics, 17*(3), 77–101.
Ministry of Finance. (2009). Report No. 2 (2009–2010) to the Storting. *Revised National Budget 2010, 2*.
Ministry of Labour and Government Administration. (2003). Proposition No. 6 (2003–2004) to the Odelsting.
Monsen, N. (2009, June 4). Regnskap o offentlig sektor, opinion piece. *Klassekampen*.
Navarro, V. (2002). A critique of social capital. *International Journal of Health Service, 32*, 424–432.
Newberry, S. (2012). Bruk av forretningsorienterte regnskaper i New Zealands sentralregjering. Oppnådde resultater og nye refleksjoner. *Fagbladet Samfunn Økonomi*, 2-2012.
Newberry, S., & Pallot, J. (2006, September). New Zealand's financial management system implications for democracy. *Public Money and Management, 26*, 221–227.
Putnam, R. D. (1993). *Making democracy work: Civic tradition in modern Italy*. Princeton, NJ: Princeton University Press.
Veggeland, N. (2009). *Taming the regulatory state: Politics and ethics*. Cheltenham: Edward Elgar Publishing.
Veggeland, N. (2010). *Den nye reguleringsstaten. Idébrytninger og styringskonflikter*. Oslo: Gyldendal Akademisk.
Veggeland, N. (2012). *Styring og reguleringsparadokser*. Trondheim: Akademisk Forlag.

Appendix A

OECD Statistical Data

Here you may find comprehensive statistical data from the OECD and the EU to your
information and use for further reading of this book:
Norway: https://data.oecd.org/norway.htm
Sweden: https://data.oecd.org/sweden.htm
Denmark: https://data.oecd.org/denmark.htm
Finland: https://data.oecd.org/finland.htm
Iceland: https://data.oecd.org/iceland.htm

Trend and Ranking in the OECD

OECD Data: Extracts Norway

Population 5.2 Million

Government	Latest	Trend	Ranking
General government spending indicator	50.8 Total % of GDP 2016 Norway % of GDP	Total % of GDP 1997–2016 Norway (red)	Total % of GDP 2016 Norway (red)

(continued)

© Springer Nature Switzerland AG 2020
N. Veggeland, *Democratic Governance in Scandinavia*,
https://doi.org/10.1007/978-3-030-18270-0

Government	Latest	Trend	Ranking
Reserves indicator	44,628.6 Total SDR millions Q4-2014 Norway SDR millions	Total SDR millions Q1-2010–Q4-2014 Norway (red)	Total SDR millions Q4-2014 Norway (red)
Profits indicator	4.6 Total % of GDP 2017 Norway % of GDP	Total % of GDP 1998–2017 Norway (red), OECD—Average (black)	Total % of GDP 2017 Norway (red), OECD—Average (black)
Revenue indicator	38.2 Total % of GDP 2017 Norway % of GDP	Total % of GDP 1998–2017 Norway (red), OECD—Average (black)	Total % of GDP 2017 Norway (red), OECD—Average (black)
Wedge indicator	35.9 Total % of labor cost 2017 Norway % of labor cost	Total % of labor cost 2000–2017 Norway (red), OECD—Average (black)	Total % of labor cost 2017 Norway (red), OECD—Average (black)

OECD Data: Extract Sweden

Population: 9.7 Millions

Government	Latest	Trend	Ranking
Spending indicator	49.7 Total % of GDP 2016 Sweden % of GDP	Total % of GDP 1997–2016 Sweden (red)	Total % of GDP 2016 Sweden (red)
Reserves indicator	39,970.3 Total SDR millions Q4-2014 Sweden SDR millions	Total SDR millions Q1-2010–Q4-2014 Sweden (red)	Total SDR millions Q4-2014 Sweden (red)
Profits indicator	2.6 Total % of GDP 2017 Sweden % of GDP	Total % of GDP 1998–2017 Sweden (red), OECD—Average (black)	Total % of GDP 2017 Sweden (red), OECD—Average (black)
Revenue indicator	44.0 Total % of GDP 2017 Sweden % of GDP	Total % of GDP 1998–2017 Sweden (red), OECD—Average (black)	Total % of GDP 2017 Sweden (red), OECD—Average (black)
Wedge indicator	42.9 Total % of labor cost 2017 Sweden % of labor cost	Total % of labor cost 2000–2017 Sweden (red), OECD—Average (black)	Total % of labor cost 2017 Sweden (red), OECD—Average (black)

OECD Data: Extract Demark

Population: 5.7 Millions

Government	Latest	Trend	Ranking
Spending indicator	52.7 Total % of GDP 2016 Denmark % of GDP	 Total % of GDP 1997–2016 Denmark (red)	 Total % of GDP 2016 Denmark (red)
Reserves indicator	50,331.0 Total SDR millions Q4–2014 Denmark SDR millions	 Total SDR millions Q1-2010–Q4-2014 Denmark (red)	 Total SDR millions Q4-2014 Denmark (red)
Profits indicator	3.0 Total % of GDP 2017 Denmark % of GDP	 Total % of GDP 1998–2017 Denmark (red), OECD—Average (black)	 Total % of GDP 2017 Denmark (red), OECD—Average (black)
Revenue indicator	46.0 Total % of GDP 2017 Denmark % of GDP	 Total % of GDP 1998–2017 Denmark (red), OECD—Average (black)	 Total % of GDP 2017 Denmark (red), OECD—Average (black)
Wedge indicator	36.3 Total % of labor cost 2017 Denmark % of labor cost	 Total % of labor cost 2000–2017 Denmark (red), OECD—Average (black)	 Total % of labor cost 2017 Denmark (red), OECD—Average (black)

OECD Data: Extract Finland

Population: 5.6 Millions

Government	Latest	Trend	Ranking
Spending indicator	55.9 Total % of GDP 2016 Finland % of GDP	Total % of GDP 1997–2016 Finland (red)	Total % of GDP 2016 Finland (red)
Reserves indicator	6111.2 Total SDR millions Q4-2014 Finland SDR millions	Total SDR millions Q1-2010–Q4-2014 Finland (red)	Total SDR millions Q4-2014 Finland (red)
Profits indicator	2.7 Total % of GDP 2017 Finland % of GDP	Total % of GDP 1998–2017 Finland (red), OECD—Average (black)	Total % of GDP 2017 Finland (red), OECD—Average (black)
Revenue indicator	43.3 Total % of GDP 2017 Finland % of GDP	Total % of GDP 1998–2017 Finland (red), OECD—Average (black)	Total % of GDP 2017 Finland (red), OECD—Average (black)
Wedge indicator	42.9 Total % of labor cost 2017 Finland % of labor cost	Total % of labor cost 2000–2017 Finland (red), OECD—Average (black)	Total % of labor cost 2017 Finland (red), OECD—Average (black)

OECD Data: Extract Iceland

Populations: 0.31 Millions

Government	Latest	Trend	Ranking
Spending indicator			
Reserves indicator	2832.2 Total SDR millions Q4-2014 Iceland SDR millions	Total SDR millions Q1-2010–Q4-2014 Iceland (red)	Total SDR millions Q4-2014 Iceland (red)
Profits indicator	2.8 Total % of GDP 2017 Iceland % of GDP	Total % of GDP 1998–2017 Iceland (red), OECD—Average (black)	Total % of GDP 2017 Iceland (red), OECD—Average (black)
Revenue indicator	37.7 Total % of GDP 2017 Iceland % of GDP	Total % of GDP 1998–2017 Iceland (red), OECD—Average (black)	Total % of GDP 2017 Iceland (red), OECD—Average (black)
Wedge indicator	33.2 Total % of labor cost 2017 Iceland % of labor cost	Total % of labor cost 2000–2017 Iceland (red), OECD—Average (black)	Total % of labor cost 2017 Iceland (red), OECD—Average (black)

Appendix B

55 Years of European Legislation

http://www.dimiter.eu/Eurlex.html
"The European Communities, destined to become the European Union we all know today, were established back in 1957 in Rome. Since, the European Union has adopted more than 100,000 (one hundred thousand) legislative acts. That's a lot of legislation! This presentation provides a closer look into the evolution of EU legislation over time". Dimiter Toshkov (2014): *"Research design in political science"*, published by *Palgrave Macmillan.*

Dimiter Toshkov, is a social scientist who studies politics, governance, and public policy. Currently he is a Jean Monnet fellow at the Robert Schuman Centre for Advanced Studies at the European University Institute in Florence and Associate Professor at the Institute of Public Administration at Leiden University in The Netherlands.

Figure below by Dimiter Toshkov *shows the number of directives, regulations and decisions adopted by the EU from 1967 till 2012.*

He writes: "EU legislation comes in three main forms: *directives (red curve), regulations (Green curve)*, and *decisions (blue curve)*, see curves below. Directives are the most important and most general of the three. There are many important regulations as well, but usually regulations have a more narrow focus and limited application time. Decisions are the least general of the three. Directives are like real laws, and regulations and decisions are like government decrees.

We see that the annual number of legislative acts adopted by the EU has been steadily growing till the mid-1990s, but afterwards the growth has slowed down, and for regulations has been reversed. Nowadays, the EU approves on average 80 directives, 1200 regulations and 700 decisions per year. Still quite a lot! And look at the wild yearly variation in the number of directives adopted after 2000!"

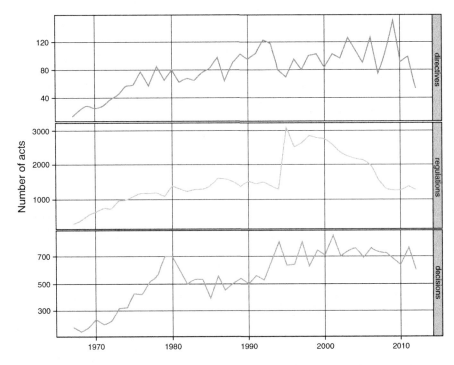

See also latest EU Data: Figures from 2018–2019 on regulatory endeavors (EU Commission):

Directives 98
Regulations 1975
Decisions 2136

Printed by Printforce, United Kingdom